THANKS

Emilie, for once again being a patient cover model, eating Swedish food for almost two years and making another drawing for this book.

Anders Ekberg, for believing in yet another book about Swedish food and traditions.

Johanna Ekberg, for her endless support and help navigating the twists and turns of book production.

My parents, Göran and Lena Lundgren, for letting me use all the family recipes and giving me a childhood full of traditions.

Mrs. Carrin M. Patman and Mr. William N Patman, for their support and encouragement in believing that this book would be interesting to Americans.

Olle Wästberg and Inger Claesson Wästberg, for their generosity in sharing their numerous Swedish-American contacts.

Stan Schwartz for a little extra translation help.

Niamh Clinton for her opinions.

To everybody who so warmly supported our first book and asked us for a sequel.

SWEDISH HOMECOOKING
© Catarina Lundgren Åström 2005
Text: Catarina Lundgren Åström
Photography: Catarina Lundgren Åström
Illustrations and photography: Peter Åström
English translation: Jennifer Brown Bäverstam
Editing: Elizabeth Levy
Graphic design: Claes Gustavsson
Production: Bokbolaget, Malmö, Sweden
Printed by: Fälth & Hässler, Värnamo, Sweden 2005

ISBN: 91-7843-198-0

Contents

Introduction 7

Spring, Lenten Buns and Other
    Good Things 10
Swedish Food 18
Spring is Here and it's Celebrated
    with Waffles 44
Easter 48
Walpurgis Eve and the First of May 61
Exams and End of School Year 78
National Day 84
Whitsuntide – a Big Holiday for Weddings 98
Midsummer and Finally Summer is Here 100
Ladies' Week 132
Crayfish 157
Autumn's Darkness Falls 166
All Saints' and Martin Goose Day 212

Measurements and Conversions 222
Index of recipes 222

Introduction

▸ When is the next book coming out? After having been asked the question enough times, my husband and I decided to do a sequel to our book, *Swedish Christmas*. It was obvious to us what its contents should be. The Swedish year in food offers so much more than just the Christmas smörgåsbord, even if the smörgåsbord does include many great dishes served the entire year round.

Now, after months of eating our way through the Swedish national cuisine, we can say this: Swedish cooking is very underrated. The food we thought was dull while growing up, since we ate it all the time, seems luxurious compared with all the hamburgers and pizzas and other half-cooked food we gulp down in vast amounts. The excuse that many Swedes give is that it is too much work to make home cooked meals. This is a myth. Many of the dishes can be prepared quickly, even if some of them require a little planning. Traditional and innovative styles of home cooking are also having a renaissance in Swedish restaurants.

History lies at the foundations of Swedish home cooking, of course. Christmas, Midsummer, crayfish festivals, fermented herring festivals, and Martin Goose Day are just a few of the other traditions we Swedes like to celebrate and share with others. That Swedish culinary creations are enjoyed at least equally well outside the borders of our country should be acknowledged. This is something that the restaurants Ulrika's and Aquavit in New York, where my husband and I live, have demonstrated. Maybe it is necessary to put a little distance between a Swede and his or her homeland for them to truly appreciate Swedish cuisine and Swedish traditions. Never before have I encountered so many Swedes who love Swedish customs and traditions as those who live outside their country or have a few generations of Swedish ancestry behind them.

To gain a little more insight I have, just as in *Swedish Christmas*, chosen to turn back to my childhood and to that curiosity with which a child looks at traditions. I have combined this with historical facts and how I as a Swede abroad today see our customs and habits. As in the previous book I have chosen to focus on the folklore and not look closely at the religious aspects.

Welcome to the table!

Spring, Lenten Buns and Other Good Things

The Christmas food has hardly been put away when Lenten buns are brought out. A Lenten bun is a pastry filled with delicious almond paste and whipped cream that we Swedes love to gorge ourselves on between Christmas and Easter. Actually, the original idea was that the buns would be eaten on Shrove Tuesday, one of the feast days just before Lent, the fast leading up to Easter, begins. But Lenten buns proved so popular bakeries began to bake them so they would appear by New Year's Day. Lenten buns, or Shrovetide buns, Shrove Tuesday buns, and hot cross buns, as these famous buns are also known, were introduced in their present form by bakeries in the 1920s. But their history goes back significantly further.

Before Martin Luther reformed the Swedish church to Protestantism in the 1500s, the country was Catholic. At that time there was an obligatory fast during the forty days preceding Easter. During this fast people couldn't eat meat or any other rich food. Stockfish was the usual meal. Life was to be uneventful, and people didn't announce an engagement or get married during this time lest they be doomed to live a life of poverty, or so superstition warned. Before Lent began, people celebrated with three days of gluttony, which was called "fastlagen" from the German "fastenabend." These days were not only devoted to food. Peo-

ple amused themselves with all kinds of games, like the popular "hit the cat in the barrel," which involved hanging a cat in a barrel from a tree. Horsemen would try to knock down the barrel with clubs and thus free the poor cat. The victor was rewarded with the title of "Cat King" for the day. In Skåne, the southernmost province, the days before Lent were named "Pork Sunday, Bun Monday and Fat Tuesday." In the northern parts of Sweden, Fat Tuesday was one of the year's biggest holidays. Then the entertainment for large and small was to tie together sleds, two by two. When people were sliding down the hills at top speed they would shout "Make way! A long line and a big tumble." The weather on Fat Tuesday was said to be a harbinger of the spring's weather. People celebrated by eating huge buns made of wheat flour, which in Latin is called "semel," from which comes "semlor," the Swedish word for Lenten buns. These buns were filled with almond paste and eaten with warm milk, which is the way many still prefer their Lenten buns, though I don't.

After some years on American soil I can say that Lenten buns are probably the only thing that I really miss, especially the Lenten buns from the Dalpojken bakery on Rörstrandsgatan in Stockholm. It was around the corner from where I lived and I wasn't the only one who loved its buns.

The evening paper often gave it top ratings when the capital city's Lenten buns were taste-tested. When I was home this past year I even succeeded in getting the baker to bake me a box of Lenten buns, although the season had long been over. He had a good laugh at my order but I got my buns, and it was with great gusto that my family and I ate them up.

You get the best Lenten buns at bakeries I believe. They have a special fluffiness that is so hard to achieve when you bake them at home. Still, I think it is much, much better to have home-baked Lenten buns than no Lenten buns at all. Everyone should taste this gourmet Swedish pastry.

Just be careful not to eat too many, or else you could end up like King Adolf Fredrik, who in 1771 died from a stroke after a meal that ended with too many Lenten buns!

Even detective Ture Sventon, a well-known children's book character, loves Lenten buns. "No Lenten buns, no assignment," is his motto of sorts, though he insists on calling them "temlor", instead of the Swedish "semlor". Either way, this festive wheat bun is absolutely worth fighting for.

LENTEN BUNS

Lenten buns, Shrovetide buns, Shrove Tuesday buns, hot cross buns: a beloved child has many names. This pastry dates back to the time when Sweden was still a Catholic country. At that time the practice was to fast for 40 days before Easter. Before beginning the fast, people would allow themselves to indulge in a few extra treats, including this wheat bun filled with almond paste. Lenten buns were consumed with delight on Shrove Tuesday (the Tuesday before Lent began).

Today the season for Lenten buns starts significantly earlier. Bakeries have Lenten buns on display by New Year's Day, and the buns are eaten with pleasure up until Easter. The average Swede is estimated to munch on 4-5 buns during that time. In the 1920s people made this an even more luxurious treat by topping the almond filling with a bit of whipped cream. Many prefer to eat Lenten buns in a bowl with warm milk. But don't try to order Lenten buns in Finland—you'll probably get just an ordinary French roll.

Makes 16 buns

2 packages active dry yeast
4 oz butter or margarine

1 1/3 cups whole milk
1/3 cup sugar
1/2 tsp. salt
1 egg
1 tsp. ground cardamom
4 cups all-purpose flour

1 egg for glazing the dough

Filling:
crumbs from the center of the buns
8 oz almond paste or marzipan
a little bit of milk
1 1/2 cups heavy cream for whipping
powdered sugar

Oven temperature: 425-450° F

- Melt the butter in a pan. Add milk when the butter is melted and warm to the touch (98°).
- Sprinkle the yeast in a mixing bowl and pour the milk mixture over it. Stir until the yeast is completely dissolved.
- Add the sugar, salt, cardamom and egg. Mix well.
- Stir in the flour until it forms a dough.
- Knead the dough for a few minutes, then cover and let rise for 30 minutes.
- Knead the dough again and divide it in two.
- Make each half into a long roll and

divide it into eight pieces.

- Form the pieces into round balls and place them on buttered baking sheet and let rise for 30 minutes.
- Brush the buns with beaten egg just before placing them in the oven.
- Bake in the middle of the oven until they have turned a golden brown.
- When the buns have cooled, cut a little lid out of the top and scrape out the inside. Crumble until it has a crumblike consistency, then mix with the almond paste or marzipan.

Add a little milk to achieve a pastelike texture.

- Fill the buns with the almond mixture.
- Add a dollop of whipped cream on top of the almond mixture and replace the lids.
- Use a sieve to sprinkle the buns with powdered sugar.
- Now the Lenten buns are ready to enjoy. If you like, you can eat them in a bowl with warm milk poured over them.

The first Sunday in February is Candlemas Day, and it was said that the more it stormed on that day, the better the year would be, if large snowdrifts lay on the ground, summer would come early. Candlemas Day was once known as "little Christmas Eve." I remember how my mother would bring out the frozen leftovers of the Christmas ham, ham stock for dipping in the pot, stockfish and rice pudding. But I think we were rather alone in keeping that tradition alive. It was all about getting to taste the Christmas delicacies and lighting some Christmas candles once more. Candlemas Day is a bright holiday that once literally lit up the winter darkness. It was on this day that wax candles were to be consecrated. These candles were considered holy and doctors in the Middle Ages strongly recommended their use for medicinal purposes.

The Swedish winter is well known for being long and dark, and every little sign of spring is gratefully received. When the blanket of snow finally melts, the first flower to peek out is usually coltsfoot. Plump and yellow, it suddenly appears. I remember that as a child I was quick to pick the first coltsfoot and hurry home to show off my find, which would be placed in an eggcup to remind everyone at the dinner table that spring was on its way. This usually occurred in the middle of February.

One year my friend Marianne found a coltsfoot at the end of January. Her mother called the local paper, which wrote a little line about it. I was green with envy. Why hadn't I

been the one to find it? I wanted to be written about. That my friend found it behind my grandfather's factory was even more humiliating. That was, after all, my coltsfoot territory!

I almost lived at the factory, where they made sweaters and other things. My grandfather had, once upon a time, started out as rover, a sort of house-to-house peddlar, who traveled around on a bicycle and sold clothing that the ladies of the village produced in their free time. There were plenty of rovers who bicycled around the Borås area in the 1930s. My grandfather, however, had bigger dreams. He wanted to build up his own business and soon he had several factories where clothing was produced at a steady rate, giving plenty of work to the village.

Both my mother and my father, all my mother's siblings, almost all of my grandfather's siblings, and several of their children worked there. I still remember the smell of yarn and newly knit wool from the thundering knitting machines. It was almost impossible to hear anything inside the factory. The only things that could cut through the din were a radio, which must have been played at an extremely high volume, and mama's voice. She worked at the reception desk and received phone calls and visitors. Now and then she would interrupt the noise with messages.

I also remember sewing on the overlock sewing machines when I was way too little. I would never have let my own daughter sew on them when she was six. But I was stubborn and thought that I could do it. I almost lived, as I said, at my grandfather's factory. There was no daycare at that time, and since both mama and papa worked, I was usually there too. I loved to tape boxes because there was a cool machine that automatically dispensed the tape when you pushed a button. My uncle used to tease me and say I couldn't use the machine until I was big enough to say "tape dispenser", which was difficult for a four-year-old.

When I wasn't playing around the factory I was usually with my grandmother, who served coffee to the customers. I liked to talk to the customers; to say I was a talkative child is an understatement. As a child I established acquaintances with people such as Erling Persson, who founded H&M. He was a loyal customer

16

and used to come visit my grandfather. When Persson opened an H&M store a few years ago in New York City's Herald Square, I ran into him and reminded him of where we used to see each other. He remembered his visits to the factory very well. Persson also told me that he stood outside Macy's in 1946, looked up at the building on the other side of the street and said to himself: "Here is where I will have my store." And now, there it stood.

If anyone had said to me when I was growing up in a little village in Västergötland that one day I would live in New York City, it would have seemed as impossible as moving to the moon. I had set my sights on Stockholm instead. I had decided on this when very young. I wanted to live in the crowds, have a big apartment downtown with high ceilings and ceramic stoves. Having a house wasn't my thing. I hated it when I had to help out at home mowing the lawn, raking the leaves and weeding. I meant it when I said I would never deal with these things when I grew up. You can avoid all of them by living in the city, so the asphalt jungle of New York suits me quite well, even if it is hard to find any coltsfoot here.

Snowdrops growing along the walls of the house were another early sign of spring in Sweden. They looked stately, standing tall with their white, drop-shaped petals. And out on the hillsides, just like in Alice Tegner's song "Blåsippan uti backarna står", the blue anemones bloomed. In Sweden there are many beautiful children's songs about the different sea-

sons, sung over and over in childhood and, presumably, never forgotten. Alice Tegnér is the woman behind many of these songs. It is rare to find places where blue anemones grow in the wild and they are therefore on a protected list. They cannot be picked; they can only be looked at. We children knew this well, so we only looked at them and instead picked lots of white wood anemones and yellow gagea flowers, which grew in the same places. In Sweden there is a unique law called right of common use. It makes it possible to walk freely out in nature and pick wild flowers (except for those that are protected, of course) and mushrooms without asking the landowner. This ensures that everyone can enjoy our fantastic countryside, and that all you have to do is pack the picnic basket, go out into the woods and throw yourself down wherever you like.

Swedish Food

▶▶ The question is whether or not there is any other country in the world where people eat as many potatoes as in Sweden, or have as many potato dishes to choose from. Boiled, fried, roasted, baked, riced, mashed, grated and fried potato pancakes and potato dumplings.... The variations are many and we should thank Jonas Alströmer, who once upon a time introduced Swedes to this beloved tuber.

Potatoes are eaten at almost every dinner in Sweden. But that doesn't mean that Swedish meals are monotonous in any way. Thanks to almost 100,000 lakes and long coastlines, fish also have a central role in Swedish home cooking. Salmon is one of the most popular fish, and it is eaten poached, smoked, fried and in salmon pudding, among other preparations. When I was a child, it was always a party when salmon was brought to the table. For a time salmon was hard to catch and a real treasure among fish. Now it is farmed in Norwegian waters and can be bought at a low price. In earlier times, salmon was unbelievably common and not at all special. Servants wrote into their contracts that they would have to eat salmon no more than four times a week. That sounds luxurious today!

If salmon was common, herring (called Baltic herring when caught in the Baltic sea) was more so. The lack of refrigeration meant that people had to preserve food some other way so it wouldn't spoil. One method was to salt the fish, another to let it ferment in a lightly-salted brine, creating what is known as fermented Baltic herring. Some consider it a delicacy; others find it completely inedible. The first time this fish appears is in the 1500s. Its home has always been along the coast in the southern part of the province of Norrland. Nowadays fermented Baltic herring is packed in cans and its season opens on the third Thursday in August.

You have to keep your distance when the cans are opened, since the smell is not the best. There are those who say Sweden won the thirty-year war thanks to fermented Baltic herring. Hungry Swedish soldiers were beside themselves with joy when they tasted their fermented herring, and ate it like fiends. Then they breathed on the enemy….

If fermented Baltic herring doesn't do anything for you, maybe pickled herring is more appealing. Herring is eaten particularly in the summer, preferably out of doors. Herring is also served at Christmas, Easter and Midsummer, and with that little shot of schnapps that is almost a signal for herring. Once upon a time gentlemen of the bourgeoisie partook of something called the "schnapps table", which often preceded larger dinners. In a corner of the room, a table was set with different kinds of herring, homemade pickled anchovies, aged cheese, and salted pretzels. With these one drank schnapps. Women usually had to be content with a lump of sugar dipped in schnapps. The schnapps table is said to be the predecessor to what is called the smörgåsbord, a table spread with all kinds of delicacies and most often found at restaurants. The only time that you find a smörgåsbord in the home is at Christmas, when a table is laden with an incomparable spread of food.

The Swedish smörgåsbord is overflowing with food, and people are meant to refill their plates at least four or five times. Mostly this is so as not to mix too many tastes. One usually begins with herring, then switches to salad and cold dishes before getting started on the warm dishes and finishing up with something sweet.

Smörgåsbords were uncommon in the old peasant society of Sweden. Peasant food was markedly meager, and it was more a question of eating at all than of eating fine foods. The dominant food was porridge. Most often it would be cooked for the evening meal, and the rest fried and eaten in the morning, with syrup in the best case. It was not a given that milk would be served with porridge; it could just as well be fish stock, meat stock or honey mixed with water. On more important holidays like Christmas white porridge was served, usually rice porridge.

In the old days meat was scarce, as livestock was mostly raised for dairy production. In the middle and northern parts of Sweden the dairymaids were sent out to the mountain pastures with the cows around Midsummer and didn't return home until fall arrived. There they produced cheeses, cooked whey-cheese, and processed buttermilk, or sour milk.

Meat was associated with festive occasions like Christmas. That was when the pig was slaughtered and people could really indulge themselves with fine food.

A meat-eating exception to the traditional Swedish diet was the men of Dalarna, who worked hard in the copper mines of Falun. King Gustav Vasa had imported manpower for the mines from Belgium and Germany. A large number of oxen also worked in the mines and when they had no more strength for hauling they were slaughtered. From this meat the "new Swedes" made a kind of sausage that they called Falu sausage, a delicacy that is still served at dinner tables throughout Sweden.

Almost everything eaten in the old days was produced on farms. A little extra could be found in the sea when you fished or in the woods when you hunted. Stores didn't appear out in the country until the 1800s, when the first small shops opened. Often people bartered goods. Stores came to the cities earlier on, and city people went to the butcher, the fishmonger and the baker when they needed to fill their larders. Even city dwellers had small pantries and cellars to store food. In the country people had earth cellars.

In the country bread was baked in bake houses where women from several farms got together and baked a bread supply for many months. Most often they baked crisp bread and thin bread, which kept extra long when dried.

In the middle of the 1800s the wood-burning stove, something that had been a privilege of the upper class, became a part of every man's household. It was a revolution for housewives. Suddenly they could prepare food easily and fried food made its debut. Before stoves, all food had been cooked over an open fire in an iron kettle that stood on three legs or hung by chains over the fire. Now meatballs and pork could be fried right in the home, and small cakes baked in ovens became a real treat to have with the coffee that was becoming more common. Before this all nourishment had been washed down with large quantities of beer and schnapps.

Wood-burning stoves expanded the creative possibilities for housewives in the kitchen, and many of the home-cooked meals still loved today came into being. Cajsa Warg's cookbook, *Helpful Housekeeping Advice for Young Wives*, came out in 1755. Swedish meatballs are, without a doubt, one of Sweden's signature national dishes, but they are also known as "mama's meatballs". The phrase was actually coined by an American. Before Ingemar Johansson won the heavyweight boxing championship against Floyd Patterson in 1959, Ingo's mother invited the gathered press for meatballs – mama's meatballs.

PEA SOUP AND PUNSCH

Thursday is the day pea soup is on the menu, a custom that also dates to when Sweden was a Catholic country. Friday was a day of fasting, so people ate a substantial meal on Thursday evening to store up reserves.

Today the Friday fast is merely a memory, but the custom of serving pea soup on Thursdays is still alive in many restaurants. The soup is typically served at lunchtime with pancakes for dessert.

The long shelf life of dried peas has made them an ideal provision for seafaring vessels and military encampments. Pea soup, in particular, seems to taste better if it is made in large amounts. There have been cases where one ate a spoonful too much, however. At Örebro Castle in 1577, King Erik XIV pea soup turned out to be poisoned with arsenic and consequently became the king's last meal.

The custom of drinking warm punsch (a kind of liqueur) with pea soup began in the eighteenth century after East Indian traders brought home the main ingredient, arrak, an alcoholic drink similar to rum. Punsch peaked in the 1800s, when more than 6 million liters were consumed each year. Today it is popular mainly in student circles. Punsch is sometimes served warm in a special little glass with a small handle.

Pea Soup

1 lb yellow split peas
7 2/3 cups water
1-1 1/2 tsp. salt
2 small yellow onions
1/2 lb salt pork
1 bay leaf
1-2 tsp. marjoram

- Soak the peas for 10-12 hours.
- Drain.
- Boil the peas with the water, salt and bay leaf.
- Peel and chop the onions.
- Cut the salt pork into cubes. (The soup can also be made with without salt pork, but then the amount of salt should be increased somewhat.)
- When the peas have cooked for about 20 minutes, add the onions and pork. Let everything simmer over low heat until the peas are soft. Stir now and then and then add the marjoram.
- Serve the soup with mustard and warm punsch if desired.

Punsch

1 cup dark Jamaican rum
1/3 cup water
3/4 cup sugar

- Boil the sugar and water until they make a syrup. Let the syrup cool.
- Combine the sugar syrup with the rum in a bottle and shake until the syrup dissolves.

- It is preferable to let the punsch stand and draw for a few days to let the flavor come out.

SWEDISH PANCAKES

Swedish pancakes have become widely known as a delicacy few can resist. They taste best warm with whipped cream and strawberry preserves. Makes approximately 12 pancakes.

3 eggs
1 1/3 cups all-purpose flour
2 2/3 cups whole milk

butter or margarine for frying

- Beat the eggs with half the milk. Add the flour and then the rest of the milk. Beat until the batter is smooth and free of lumps.

- Heat a frying pan and add butter, letting it brown slightly.
- Pour about 1/3 cup batter into the pan. Tilt the pan until a thin layer covers the whole bottom.
- When the batter on the side facing up is no longer runny, flip the pancake over and let that side get a little color.

MEAT WITH DILL SAUCE

Lamb, veal or beef: all go equally well with this tart, refreshing sauce seasoned with fresh dill.

2.5 lb. lamb, veal or beef
4 cups water
1 tsp. salt
a pinch of white pepper
a few sprigs of dill

- Cut the meat into approx. one-inch cubes.
- Bring the meat to a boil in the water and then simmer over a low heat for 1 -1 1/2 hours in a covered saucepan.
- Add the salt, white pepper and dill sprigs and let it boil together with the meat.

Dill Sauce

1 tbsp. butter or margarine
2 tbsp. flour
1 tsp. sugar
1/3 cup chopped dill
1-2 tbsp. freshly squeezed lemon juice
2 cups of the meat stock, adding a little water if there isn't enough

- Strain the meat stock.
- Melt the butter in a saucepan and add the flour. Make sure it is well blended. Thin with the meat stock, a little at a time. Stir so that the sauce thickens.
- Add the dill, the squeezed lemon juice, and the sugar, and let it cook slowly for a few minutes.
- Adjust the seasoning, adding salt and pepper if necessary, and pour the sauce over the meat. Garnish with lemon slices.

SWEDISH SANDWICHES

Shrimp with egg and mayonnaise, eggs with anchovies or matjes herring, meatballs with red beet salad; these are three classic Swedish sandwiches that are commonly served at cafés.

The Swedish sandwich culture differs from that of other parts of the world, as Swedish sandwiches are usually served open-faced. There is a larger version of the sandwich called a "gangway" that features a combination of different toppings. Sandwich tortes, which, as the name implies, are tortes made up of sandwich ingredients are also consumed with enthusiasm in Sweden. These consist of several layers of bread with fillings between. The sandwich torte is covered with a layer of mayonnaise blended with whipped cream and is usually garnished with shrimp and caviar.

Personally, I find the sandwich torte a little too rich and prefer to eat a regular sandwich with egg, shrimp or meatballs on a slice of Swedish sweet limpa bread.

Shrimp Sandwich

Per person

1 egg
6-8 oz. cooked small shrimp
1 slice bread
butter
mayonnaise
sprig of dill
slice of lemon

- Hard-boil the egg.
- Butter the bread.
- Slice the egg and arrange it on the bread.
- Place a dollop of mayonnaise on top.
- Peel the cooked shrimp, if necessary, and pile them on the sandwich in a little mound.
- Garnish with the lemon slice and the dill sprig.

Pickled Beets

2 cans of sliced beets
2 cups water
3/4 cup sugar
3/4 cup 5 % distilled vinegar
a pinch ground white pepper
5 whole cloves

- Bring the water, vinegar, sugar and spices to the boil until the sugar has melted to a syrup.
- Leave to cool.
- Put the slices of red beets in a glass jar.
- Pour in the pickling liquid.
- Store in the fridge.

Meatball Sandwich with Red Beet Salad

    meatballs (see recipe on p. 34)
    red beet salad (see right)
    1 slice bread
    butter
    sprig of parsley

- Butter the bread.
- Place a layer of red beet salad on a slice of bread.
- Slice the meatballs and arrange on the bread.
- Garnish with a little sprig of parsley.

Red Beet Salad

    Approximately 25 slices pickled red beets (see recipe on p. 30)

    3 tbsp. mayonnaise

- Dice the pickled beets fine.
- Place them in a bowl and stir in the mayonnaise.
- Add a few drops of the red beet brine to give the salad a little color.

Egg Sandwich with Matjes Herring

    1 egg
    1 slice bread
    butter
    a few pieces of Matjes herring

- Hard-boil the egg.
- Butter the bread.
- Slice the egg and lay it on the bread.
- Garnish with the bits of herring.

Sweet Limpa Bread

    2 cups lukewarm water (98° F)
    2 packages active dry yeast
    2/3 cup brown sugar
    2 eggs
    4 1/2-5 cups all-purpose flour
    1 1/4 cups rye flour
    1-2 tsp. fennel seed, optional

Oven temperature: 350° F

- Stir the yeast in the warm water. Make sure it is all dissolved.
- Add the brown sugar, fennel seeds (optional) and the beaten eggs. Stir.
- Blend the rye flour and the all-purpose flour in a bowl. Add the flour mixture to the liquid, stirring until it forms a dough.
- Knead the dough for a few minutes, then cover and let rise for 30-45 minutes.
- Knead the dough again for a few minutes.
- Divide the dough in two and form loaves.
- Let the loaves rise on a baking sheet until almost double in size.
- Bake the bread in the oven. Fill a steel-handled pan with water and place it in the bottom of the oven. This will cause steam to build up in the oven, making the bread extra crisp.
- Bake the bread about 30 minutes, until it has a good brown color.

32

MEATBALLS WITH CREAM GRAVY

It doesn't get more Swedish than this. Meatballs with mashed potatoes, cream gravy and lingonberry preserves: a meal that it is hard to get enough of, even as a Swede. We can thank Ikea for spreading it all over the world and making it popular even outside Sweden. More meatballs are eaten in the furniture giant's restaurants than anywhere else. The secret to success in making meatballs is said to be the right balance between ground beef and ground pork.

Lingonberries are a delicacy often called "the red gold of the woods". Lingonberries have been a part of Swedish life for centuries. They were once an intrinsic part of peasant society, not least for their natural preservative, benzoic acid, which makes them extra long-lasting. This was a valuable trait when there were no freezers to be had.

Makes about 50 meatballs

1 lb ground beef, or 1/2 lb. ground
beef and 1/2 lb. ground pork
1 medium onion
1 egg
1/4 cup breadcrumbs
3 tbsp. whole milk
1/2 tsp. salt
1/4 tsp. black pepper

butter or margarine for browning

For the gravy

1 cup pan broth
1 cup heavy cream or whole milk
2 tbsp. all-purpose flour
soy sauce
salt and pepper

- Peel the onion and grate it finely
  with a grater or a food processor.
- Mix all the ingredients together in a
  bowl and work them thoroughly
  with your hands.
- Roll into meatballs in the palm of
  your hand.
- Heat butter in frying pan. Brown
  meatballs in batches.
- Reserve the fat drippings after every
  batch.

- After the last batch is cooked, leave
  (or add back) a little of the fat and
  add approximately 1 cup water.
  Cook until it forms a pan broth.
- Strain the pan broth.
- Add back approx 1/2 cup broth to a
  saucepan over low heat and whisk in
  the flour.
- Alternate adding the remaining pan
  broth and the cream or whole milk
  then simmer until gravy reaches the
  desired consistency.
- Season with soy sauce, salt and pepper to taste.

Mashed Potatoes

10-12 potatoes
water and salt
2 tbsp. butter
approx. 1 cup whole milk
salt and white pepper

- Cook and drain potatoes. Mash with
  butter.
- Add milk and continue to mash
  until they reach the desired consistency.
- Season with salt and pepper.

BAKED POTATOES WITH SHRIMP SKAGEN

This is a much loved concoction that works equally well on sandwiches or as a topping for potatoes. It was created by the legendary Swedish gastronome, Tore Wretman during a sailing race on the open sea. Toast Skagen was served at his restaurant, Riche, for the first time in 1958. Shrimp Skagen has since become Toast Skagen's closest relative. The only difference is that dill is used as a garish for Toast Skagen while it is chopped up and blended into Shrimp Skagen.

This is a very popular dish that goes equally well with toast or potatoes.

6 oz peeled, cooked shrimp
1/2 medium red onion
2 oz red caviar
2/3 cup mayonnaise
2/3 cup sour cream
dill
salt

One large baked potato per person
Alternatively, one slice of toast per person

- Peel the shrimp.
- Finely chop the onions.
- Mix the mayonnaise and the sour cream in a bowl. Add the onions and the shrimp.
- Carefully stir in the caviar.
- Finely chop or snip the desired amount of dill and blend in.
- Add salt according to taste.

RHUBARB PIE

Rhubarb was usually the first to peek out in our vegetable patch. It meant rhubarb cream and rhubarb pie. Tart and delicious, rhubarb pie was something I loved as a child and my daughter seems to have inherited a taste for it, too. Unfortunately we have no vegetable patch to grow rhubarb in, so we have to content ourselves with looking for it in the farmers' market in Union Square.

1 lb rhubarb
1/2 cup sugar

Crumb crust

1 cup all-purpose flour
1 tbsp. sugar
4 oz butter or margarine

Oven temperature: 425° F

- Begin by making the crumb crust. Combine the flour and sugar and, using a fork or your fingers, cut in the butter or margarine until the dough has a crumb-like texture. It is not supposed to stick together.
- If the rhubarb is tough, peel it, then chop into approx 1/2-inch piece
- Butter an ovenproof pie pan.
- Place the rhubarb in the pan and sprinkle sugar on top.
- Crumble a layer of dough over the rhubarb pieces and bake until golden brown.
- Serve with warm vanilla sauce (recipe on page 173) or whipped cream.

RHUBARB CREAM

1 1/2 lb rhubarb
2 cups water
2/3 cup sugar
3 tbsp. cornstarch

- Rinse rhubarb and peel if it is tough.
- Chop the rhubarb into approx 1/2-inch pieces.
- Combine the water and sugar in a saucepan, add rhubarb and bring it to a boil. Then let it simmer over medium heat, stirring now and then.
- When the rhubarb is soft, mix the cornstarch with a little water to make a liquidy paste and stir into the rhubarb mixture in the saucepan. Continue stirring until the mixture is thick and creamy.
- Serve it warm or cold with milk poured over it.

GENTLEMEN'S DELIGHT

Just like Shrimp Skagen, Gentlemen's Delight is enormously popular. Neither of these dishes is particularly complicated to make, and both usually make a lasting impression on guests. Gentlemen's Delight has always been considered a fine accompaniment for aquavit. It is especially popular as a late night snack, the perfect complement to a nightcap after hours.

6 oz Matjes herring
2-3 tbsp. brine from the Matjes herring
4 hard-boiled eggs
1 large yellow onion
black pepper
chopped parsley
butter or margarine for sautéing
brown bread or toast

- Hard-boil the eggs and chop finely.
- Drain and mince the Matjes herring into small pieces. Reserve the brine.
- Chop the onion and sauté in butter over low heat for 5 minutes.
- Toss all the ingredients together in a dish, including the reserved brine.
- Season with pepper and chopped parsley.
- Gentlemen's Delight tastes best served on a slice of thin, dark bread, but toast will work as well.

41

Spring is Here and it's Celebrated with Waffles

Spring arrives slowly in Sweden. Even on the Feast of the Annunciation on March 25 the snow is hardly ever gone completely, at least not in the northern latitudes.

Annunciation Day is also the day when the spring equinox falls, which means that day and night are equally long. This was the traditional day to begin spring planting. The cows were let out for spring grazing, and children could run around without shoes and socks if they wanted and weather permitted.

Annunciation Day was also known as the Feast Day of Our Lady, which for a long time was the last of what were once many feast days for the Virgin Mary. In 1953 even this feast day of the Virgin ceased to be a holiday. In the 1500s, when Sweden was still Catholic, almost one third of all the days of the year were feast days, something that the Protestants quickly changed. The change wasn't especially popular since the feast days were much anticipated to lighten up the tedium of everyday life. When King Gustav III came to power (1771), he took away even more feast days. After that the number remained pretty constant, though some have had to make way for others.

The Feast of Our Lady has come to be called "Waffle Day", as the names sound similar in Swedish. Waffles are something we inhabitants of the north seem to like. They are a variation on Swedish pancakes, and are baked in special waffle irons that are preferably in the form of five small hearts. You can find this kind of waffle iron even on American soil, as I recently discovered to my great joy. Until I found the heart-shaped iron, we only had a waffle iron for gigantic Belgian waffles, which didn't suit my taste at all.

Waffles are something I learned to appreciate early on, preferably eaten with cloudberry preserves. The cloudberry is a yellow berry that grows in bogs, mostly in the northern parts of Sweden, but actually also in the bogs of Västergötland, where I grew up. I remember my father would set out early in the morning with his old military backpack to pick cloudberries. Cloudberries are sometimes called "forest's gold" since their price is significantly higher

44

than that of other berries. It takes patience to pick these berries, which have a distinctive taste when they are ripe.

There are loads of ways to prepare waffles and my mother used to always make two different kinds, one so-called "crispy waffle", which, like the name says, was really crispy since the batter was largely composed of cream. The other kind was more pancake-like. As a child I thought the batter was almost as good as the waffles, and so the amount of batter in the bowl would slowly sink as I sampled it; this always perplexed my mother, who wondered if she had really made so little batter.

When I later moved to Norway I realized I had landed in "waffle paradise". Norwegians make waffles all the time, in fact almost every day. One year I worked at the National Hospital, and there the patients were provided with "freshly fried" waffles every day. While there I also learned how to prepare waffles in a significantly healthier way than my mother did. Norwegian waffles are made with soda, buttermilk (which is a sort of low-fat variation of sour cream), and oatmeal. The waffles turned out heavenly: fluffy and delicious. I have to confess that Norwegian waffles actually taste even better than Swedish ones. For this reason I now serve only Norwegian waffles. To my great joy cloudberry preserves are actually available on this side of the Atlantic, in Scandinavian stores and well-stocked food stores.

WAFFLES

Belgian waffles, American waffles, why not Swedish waffles, or rather, Norwegian? After having spent a year in Norway I couldn't resist adopting their waffles. Ever since I was a child I have loved waffles and not only on Waffle Day, which falls on March 25. Actually the Day of Our Lady falls on that date, but since "Day of Our Lady" sounds a lot like "Waffle Day" in Swedish it has been transformed over the years. People have eaten waffles in Sweden since the 1600s. I can't say whether the waffles of yore were healthy to eat or not. However, I can say that my mother's crispy waffles contained way too much cream to be eaten very often, so we had to enjoy them when we had the chance. When I went to Norway I got to eat as many waffles as I wanted, since we made them every day at the National Hospital. The fact is that Norwegian waffles are considerably more nutritious than Swedish waffles. They use sour cream, almost no fat at all and absolutely no cream, not even on top. Below is the recipe, which by now I have shared with almost everyone I know. They all agree – Norway is the best, at least when it comes to making waffles.

Makes about 6-8 waffles

3 eggs
1 1/4 cups whole milk
1/2 cup sour cream
2 cups all-purpose flour
1/2 cup Sprite or Seven Up
2 tbsp. sugar
1 tsp. baking powder

butter or margarine for baking the waffles

- Break three eggs into a bowl. Blend in the sour cream, flour, baking powder, sugar and half of the milk.
- Gradually add the rest of the milk and the soda.
- Mix until smooth.
- Melt the butter in the waffle iron and cook the waffles.
- Serve with whipped cream and strawberry, raspberry or cloudberry preserves.

Easter

▸▸ Easter has a number of things in common with Christmas, even if it doesn't involve the same amount of cleaning and decorating as before Christmas. Still, Easter cards are sent, Easter decorations are hung up, and many houses and homes are decorated with little chicks, hens and roosters. The home glows with yellow, which is so typical for Easter. Why this is no one really knows, but people have probably been inspired by chickens, Easter lilies, egg yolks and other yellow things. The food differs from Christmas in that people eat lots of eggs. This is a custom that has survived from when people fasted during Lent, when eating eggs was forbidden. So, of course, it was naturally a little festive when you could begin eating them again. There would be plenty of eggs as the hens would have just started laying well again. Eggs were not only good for eating. In Skåne, Sweden's southernmost province, people would play with eggs as well. People still have egg contests there, bumping two eggs against each other, with the one whose egg doesn't crack winning, and egg rolling.

There is no tree to decorate for Easter but people do put up Easter branches decorated with feathers in loud colors. The type of branches varies, but the most common is birch, which is seen as having divine power. In America I usually choose pussy willows with their sweet little fuzzy buds that make me think of the song "Sleep little pussy willow, for it is still winter," yet another in a long line of childhood songs that have a strong hold in my memory. People choose to put out Easter branches long before Easter, and they are usually called Lenten branches. A long time ago the custom was to hit each other with birch branches on the Monday before Lent or on Shrove Tuesday, and the key was to be quick and run off without being caught, otherwise you had to invite everyone for coffee and buns.

Nowadays Lenten branches or Easter branches are more tied in with Easter decorations. The colorful feathers in the branches are a joy for the eye, especially when they are sold in the town markets and the feathers wave in the wind. Lenten branches or Easter branches with their fine feathers were already being sold

48

in the 1800s, and people would sometimes place in them small presents or love poems to their beloved. In medieval times the branches were considered to have healing powers.

Easter week is a movable holiday; whether it falls in March or April is dependent on the moon. Easter day is always celebrated on the first Sunday after the first full moon after March 20.

As a child I was fascinated by the unusual names for the days of Easter Week, also known as Holy Week. In Swedish these were: Black Monday, White Tuesday, Damper Wednesday, Cleansing Thursday, and Long Friday. During Holy Week, there was no normal bell ringing on Thursday. Instead, the metal clapper was replaced by a wooden one, called a damper, which dampened the ring. All heavy work had to be avoided, lest terrible things

happen. It was considered extra dangerous to chop wood. People also had to avoid anything with circular movements, such as wagons, spinning wheels, etc. Cleansing Thursday got its name from an old word meaning "to purify". Long Friday was, like its name, an appallingly long and dreary day on which you had to keep quiet. All the way up to 1969 it was forbidden to organize public entertainment, and stores were closed. Today, it has eased up some; but it is still a very quiet day.

When I was a child, we always spent Easter at my grandfather's summer house in Tylösand, on the west coast in the province of Halland. The house was old, and had a large English styled fireplace that was kept lighted from morning to evening to keep away the winter chill. I remember that we had to spread out all our bedclothes so they could be warmed up

49

before it was time to go to bed. It was a wonderful house, full of nooks and crannies, and added on to a number of times. Unfortunately, the house burned down when I was only four, but the memories of it are numerous, oddly enough. What concerned me most when I heard about the disastrous fire was the fate of my own house. My grandfather had built a playhouse for me with a chimney and everything I loved. When he began to build it, he said it was going to be a garage and I couldn't quite figure it out. It was so small the car wouldn't even be able to fit into it, and besides, it began to look more and more like a playhouse, which is exactly what it turned out to be, to my great joy. The playhouse survived and Grandfather's house was rebuilt after the fire. Our family's Easter celebrations continued. A favorite tradition was going out to view the Easter bonfires on Easter Eve. This is a tradition only found in the provinces of Västergötland, Halland, Dalsland, and Värmland. In the rest of the country people save the branches from spring pruning until it is time to light the May bonfires on Walpurgis Eve, which I will come to later.

In former times, Easter bonfires were lit to drive away trolls and Easter witches, and the practice survives in the form of rockets and Easter firecrackers.

Easter firecrackers were a dangerous amusement during the weeks before Easter. There were many varieties and strengths of these Easter firecrackers. The ones that I remember most were Chinese puffs that cost about ten cents a piece and made a real bang. I usually kept to a cheaper variety with a more modest pop, though I still thought it was frightening to light them. You had to be really quick. Today, with adult eyes, I can't comprehend that we were allowed to have Easter firecrackers. We were very little, had just started school, and could hardly light the matches!

To be really honest I didn't think Easter firecrackers were that much fun. So it was with no great regret that I agreed to give them up in exchange for a record I had been wanting. The record was called "Ring-Ring" and was recorded by a pop group made up of four members: Agneta, Annifrid, Björn, and Benny. One year later the group changed their name, using the first initials of their given names, and became ABBA. What happened next is widely known. But for me they were actually my idols before they made "Waterloo." I will never forget the evening when they captured the victory at the Eurovision Song Contest in Brighton. I couldn't sleep all night.

Several years later I went to Brighton to take a language course, and of course you know the reason I chose Brighton. Many, many years later I got to meet Björn and Benny when they had a premier of the musical "Mama Mia" in New York, and together with the Swedish press they raised their glasses to their success. For even if today they are megastars, they were still eager to meet the Swedish press as soon as the curtain had gone down.

I had actually met them earlier when "Ring-Ring" came out. At that time they were traveling around with something called "People in the Park". In almost every Swedish town they had a "People's Park" with a stage and all the popular artists came when they were out on the "People in the Parks" tour. Even the future ABBA did this. I was beside myself with joy when I got their autographs, which I still have in my dresser drawer. My daughter likes to look at them because now she's a big ABBA fan. I'm sure it's thanks to "Mama Mia," which has once again brought the group to life, but they're the same group that I spent a whole Easter listening to, forgetting almost everything else about Easter.

One thing we wouldn't want to forget, of course—Easter eggs. In Sweden children are given eggs made of paper that can be opened and filled with candy. On the outside the eggs are either decorated with chickens and other Easter motifs or covered with metallic foils of different colors and tied with a bow. I'll never forget the Easter egg that my mother's cousin Lasse gave me when I was a child. It was probably the biggest Easter egg I'd ever laid eyes on, with tons of small candies that lasted all Easter. Today, it is my mother who sends Easter eggs from Sweden in the mail so that our daughter can have the chance to participate in this Swedish tradition.

Not only are candy eggs a part of Easter, but we also eat a lot of real eggs, after painting the shells, of course. Painting eggs is a custom that we adopted from the continent. Either we colored the eggs by boiling them with onions or something else that gave them color, or we chose to decorate them with watercolors and

crayons. Since my husband is a professional artist, and my daughter seems to have inherited his talent, our eggs end up being real works of art.

Food plays a central role in most Swedish festivities and Easter is no exception. Lamb is eaten on Easter, and there are probably not many homes that don't keep that tradition, though it is a relatively new one. On Good Friday there's usually salmon on the menu. Smoked, gravlax, poached or sautéed, it varies from home to home. In our home, it was poached salmon and it still is. My grandfather used to go to his local fishmonger, who had a little shop that was no more than a small stone cellar with a door. It was, by the way, the same fishmonger that Prince Bertil usually used. He had his summerhouse in Tylösand too. Not infrequently we would bump into the Prince when he was out buying his salmon. Halmstad, which lies beside Tylösand, has always been known as a salmon haunt, with the Nissan river running through town, meeting the sea right in the harbor of Halmstad. For a time it wasn't always so easy to get hold of genuine Halmstad salmon, but my grandfather was in with the fisherman, and he always made sure we got a share, which we ate poached with hollandaise sauce, accompanied by boiled potatoes, and asparagus.

At that time, lamb was not something we usually ate. Instead, my grandfather took us all to Hemmeslöv Inn outside Båstad, which is best known for tennis. Every year, the Swedish Open is played there, and Björn Borg was for many years Båstad's biggest attraction. Easter smörgåsbord was also served up at the Hemmeslöv Inn, in roughly the same way that a Christmas smörgåsbord was served, with different kinds of herring and salmon, eggs, even lamb.

Right after lunch at the inn, it was time to dress up like Easter witches, with brooms, coffee pots, cats, and scarves on our heads. The place was usually crawling with cute little Easter witches. Unfortunately the history surrounding Easter witches is considerably darker. During the 1600s, about 300 women, as well as a few men, were accused of being witches and burned at the stake. According to folklore, Cleansing Thursday was a dangerous night, when the witches traveled to Blue Hill for a banquet with the Devil himself as host. There, everything was done backwards. Everyone sat with their backs to the gigantic, long table without end, and ate with their left hands over their left shoulders. Delicious steaks and sausages were washed down with wine. At least, that was what they believed. In reality, they were served turtles, frogs, and snakes, and muddy water in their glasses, for the Devil in his wickedness had transformed their vision.

Many of the women who were charged with being witches were actually independent-minded women, who knew too much about herbs and the art of healing, and therefore were a threat to those in power and considered dangerous. They were easily blamed if something went wrong. If a cow suddenly stop-ped giving milk, the neighbor's wife might be blamed for being a witch and casting a spell on it. Distrust was widespread at that time, as was superstition. For example, it was considered important to close the flue above the fireplace so witches couldn't come down the chimney.

One year, we made a brave effort to celebrate Easter in our house on Gotland, which is Sweden's largest island and lies east of Sweden in the Baltic Sea, a wonderfully beautiful island neighboring the island of Fårö, where Ingmar Bergman lives most of the time.

It was cold when we landed and there was still snow on the ground, which we heated up and used for dishwater. We had to get drinking water from our neighbor, since our pipes were frozen and it was impossible to turn on the water. We had to light fires in the ceramic ovens round the clock to keep some semblance of warmth, and even then we had to wear our heavy clothes. But we managed to prepare our Easter lamb and eat our Easter lunch with colored eggs and herring, and it was actually very cozy, so there's a good chance we'll do it again.

In America we try to combine Swedish and American traditions. We usually have both Easter lamb and salmon, as well as various kinds of herring together with painted eggs and, of course, a little schnapps.

After all food the Easter Parade on Fifth Avenue is an obvious must. Then we are usually Swedish in that we celebrate an extra holiday. In Sweden, even Monday is a holiday – the second day of Easter.

LEG OF LAMB WITH POTATOES AU GRATIN

In Sweden, almost everybody eats lamb at Easter these days. It used to be otherwise, mainly because Easter was too early for slaughtering domestic lambs. Now lamb is imported from New Zealand to meet Swedish demand at Easter.

Leg of Lamb

5 lb leg of lamb
1/4 cup olive oil
2-3 cloves garlic
1 tsp. salt
black pepper
a sprig of rosemary

Oven temperature: 350° F

- Combine the olive oil, salt, black pepper and pressed garlic in a small bowl. Finely snip the rosemary into the bowl.
- Butter an ovenproof roasting pan.
- Trim off any excess fat from the lamb and place in buttered roasting pan.
- Rub the olive oil mixture on the lamb on all sides.
- Wrap the lamb with aluminum foil and insert a meat thermometer in the center of the leg. Make sure it doesn't touch the bone.
- Roast in the oven until the meat thermometer reaches 145° F for rare, 160° F for medium or 170° F for well done.

Gravy

pan juices from the roast
1 tbsp. flour
a little whole milk
salt

- Drain off the pan juices from the roast into a saucepan.
- Whisk in the flour to create a gravy; and heat up the gravy that is formed.
- Add milk and salt according to taste.

Potatoes au Gratin

8-10 potatoes
1-2 yellow onions
1 tsp. salt
black pepper
2 cloves garlic
1 cup mixed whole milk and cream: (2/3 cup milk + 1/3 cup heavy cream)
1/4 cup whole milk , for pouring over the casserole just before removing it from the oven

Oven temperature: 425° F

- Butter an ovenproof dish.
- Peel and thinly slice the potatoes.

Rinse them under running water to wash away the starch released when they are peeled.

- Peel and slice the onions into half rings.
- Layer the potatoes and onion in the dish, alternating a layer of potatoes with a layer of onions adding salt and pepper between the layers. Make sure that the bottom and top layers are potatoes.
- Mince the garlic (or use a garlic press) and add it to the milk and cream mixture.
- Pour the milk and cream mixture over the potatoes and cover the dish with aluminum foil.
- Bake for 20-30 minutes, then remove the foil. Let the gratin remain in the oven 20 minutes longer. When the potatoes are soft the gratin is ready. If it still hasn't browned lightly after 20 minutes, let it stay in the oven until it has a nice color. Pour 1/4 cup milk over the gratin a few minutes before taking it out of the oven.

EGG TODDY

Making egg toddy is an Easter tradition.

Per person

    1 egg yolk
    3-4 tsp. sugar
    2/3 cup boiling water, optional
    cognac, optional

- Beat the egg yolk with the sugar with a spoon directly in the glass you are serving it in. Beat until the sugar turns white and frothy.
- Season if desired with cognac. Add boiling water if you wish.

Walpurgis Eve and the First of May

▶▶ At the end of April people finally begin to see the hope of warmth and light returning after a long, cold winter. Naturally, this is something that has to be celebrated, so the thirtieth of April, Walpurgis Eve, is a holiday dedicated to the arrival of spring. As evening falls, bonfires are lit all around the country. In the warmth and glow of the fires people sing songs welcoming spring, make speeches and raise toasts to spring. During my twenty years in Stockholm I, along with thousands of other Stockholmers, usually went to the island of Riddarholmen, where a giant bonfire was lit at dusk. The atmosphere was unbelievable – just to stand at the edge of the water and watch the fading light with City Hall in the background, while feeling the warmth of the Walpurgis Eve bonfire and listening to beautiful singing.

In contrast to Easter bonfires, which are lit only in a few parts of the country, the tradition of May bonfires, which is another name for Walpurgis Eve bonfires, spread across the whole country. The first May bonfires were held in the center of Sweden in the 1700s. One reason given for lighting them is that people wanted to scare away wild animals so that they could safely let their livestock out for spring grazing.

Some miles north of Stockholm, in the university town of Uppsala, people don't only light Walpurgis Eve bonfires. At three o'clock in the afternoon, thousands of people in white student caps (the Swedish version of graduation hats) gather and run down Carolina Hill. Before this event, people have partaken of a hearty breakfast of herring and aquavit.

St. Walpurgis has given her name to this holiday, although actually Walpurgis Day falls on the first of May. But as we do so often in Sweden, we choose to jump the gun by celebrating on the eve of the actual holiday. St. Walpurgis was a missionary in Germany in the 1700s, and eventually became an abbess.

In its earliest days, a banquet was held on Walpurgis Day and people came together to repair farm fences and other things before the animals were let out to graze freely. The day ended with sucking marrow out of the leftover bones, which was thought to help maintain good health. In the 1400s and 1500s, many towns organized a large festival with a lot of play-acting. During the festivities, someone was crowned the Count of May with a large wreath of leaves, and in the countryside of southern Sweden people entertained themselves by going from house to house singing May songs on Walpurgis eve, often together with too much aquavit, which was not appreciated by everyone.

King Carl Gustav XVI's birthday happens to fall on Walpurgis Eve, a coincidence that does not go unacknowledged. At 12:15 PM, at the changing of the guard, the king comes down into the courtyard of the palace to receive the good wishes of his people and a drawing here and there from the many children who have been patiently waiting hour after hour for a glimpse of him. He then goes up to the balcony where the rest of his family is standing and waiting and all the gathered people sing "Happy Birthday" in unison. On the palace rooftop a three-sided flag flutters with the national coat of arms. It is raised every day the king is in residence and its absence is conspicuous when he's away. According to Swedish custom the flag is taken down when the sun sets.

Even though spring is being sung in on Walpurgis Eve, it's usually really cold that evening, or perhaps the cold ones are just the evenings one remembers. May 1st, however, is usually a true spring day and several times I have ended up sitting and baking myself in the sun on the rocks of central Stockholm. May 1st has been, since 1939, a holiday and a worker's day, so there are many demonstrations with red banners and marching bands all over the country, protesting injustices and such. These days the demonstration parades are considerably smaller than in 1890 when the first May Day demonstration marched away from Gärdet. The will to fight seems to have dissipated as workers' rights have improved, and these days it is quite common to invite well-known performers to the demonstrations to attract audience and participants.

Fooling others is also permitted on May 1st, even if not as many people do it as on April 1st. I remember how, as a child, I was unbelievably proud when I could finally get an adult to believe whatever unbelievable story I came up with and could call out the chant "May, May moon, I can fool you all the way to Skåne!"

April Fool's Day is still the big day for fooling people. On April Fool's even newspapers and television come out with incredible stories. One of Sweden's best-remembered jokes was played in 1962 when Swedish Television claimed that if you simply put a nylon stocking over a black and white television set, you would suddenly be able to see the broadcast in color. Many people tried this; unfortunately it didn't really work. The verse you call out to the victims of your joke is. "April, April, you stupid herring, I can trick you whenever I want." The exact origin of this expression isn't known, but fish-themed rhymes are popular all over Europe.

No one knows for certain when the custom of fooling others on April 1ˢᵗ began, but signs of it have been traced all the way back to the 1600s. One of the better-known pranks of yore happened in 1742 in the parish of Västergötland, where a false message was sent around that communion would begin earlier than usual. It caused great anger when the prank was brought to light.

When I was a child, a few weeks before May 1ˢᵗ, we used to go about selling May Flowers, small plastic flowers with a pin that allowed you to stick them in your collar. The colors of these May Flowers changed from year to year, so people started collecting them. I remember especially well an old lady who lived in our village, Tant Olga. She was a little bit of a recluse, and it felt like a small triumph to sell her May Flowers because she always brought out her large collection. Tant Olga had every single May Flower sold since the tradition began in 1907. The earliest ones were made out of paper and the hand of time had made them brittle. But they were very beautiful, I remember. I would look at them and sigh. "Imagine if I had all those!".

May Flowers was founded by Beda Hallberg, a lady who often participated in all kinds of philanthropy in turn of the century Göte-

borg. She got the idea for May Flowers from school children selling flowers to buy clothes for poor children. The profits from Beda Hallberg's flowers went instead to help those stricken with a terrible, common disease of the time, tuberculosis. Thankfully, that disease is rarely seen today, and since 1977 the earnings from selling May Flowers have gone to handicapped children. In the 1920s the program was even introduced in the U.S. under the name "Swedish Mayflower." But it wasn't as great a success as in Sweden, where every year hundreds of thousands are sold. Today you can even buy May Flowers in small wreaths or in larger sizes to put on your car. Over the years I have tried to increase my collection but unfortunately it's still pretty meager. I can't help wondering what happened to Tant Olga's unique collection.

WALLENBERGERS

This luxury version of meatballs was born, not unexpectedly, at home in the kitchen of the Wallenberg banking family. Mrs. Amalia Wallenberg, who, by the way, was the daughter of the legendary cookbook author, Dr. Hagdahl, was the one who came up with the idea of combining ground veal with egg yolks and cream to allow the meat patties to dissolve more easily in the mouth.

Wallenbergers not only taste richer, they are also larger than ordinary meatballs and they are served with lingonberry preserves, green peas and mashed potatoes.

1 lb ground veal
3/4 cup heavy cream
4 egg yolks
1 tsp. salt
1/3 tsp. white pepper
breadcrumbs

butter for sautéing

- Combine the cream with ground veal.
- Add the egg yolks one at a time until well blended.
- Season mixture with salt and pepper.
- Form eight flat patties and coat each with breadcrumbs.
- Sauté patties in butter for three minutes on each side.

BEEFSTEAK WITH ONIONS

This was my favorite meal as a child. I could eat beefsteak with onions every day and never get tired of it. Beef was also probably the first word I learned to spell. When my grandfather slaughtered a cow late every fall, I would help write "beef" on the plastic bags that we used to freeze the cuts of meat in.

1 lb round steak in thin slices
2 large yellow onions
salt
white pepper

butter or margarine for cooking

- Peel and thinly slice the onions.
- Slowly brown the onions in the butter.
- Remove the onions from the pan and keep warm.

- Turn up the heat and quickly sauté the beef on both sides in the hot pan. Salt and pepper to taste.
- Stir a little hot water into the pan with a whisk to release the pan juices, and pour over the steaks.
- Serve the steaks with the sautéed onions and boiled potatoes. Lingonberry preserves are an excellent garnish.

ROYAL POT ROAST

Sunday dinner with the good china and the whole family gathered around a royal pot roast was a tradition that survived a long time in Sweden. Unfortunately, Sunday is no longer the day of rest it once was; there are a lot of other activities to fill what has really become a second Saturday, making the fancy Sunday dinner almost unheard of today.

I liked Sunday dinner as a child, especially the gravy, which was delicious, and the game meats we often had. We sometimes had moose in the fall, since my grandfather had land where moose was hunted.

A royal pot roast should actually be prepared with anchovies, but I have left them out because it is so hard to find Swedish anchovies in brine. Anchovies in oil don't work. Fruit preserve, preferably currant jelly, and pickled pressed cucumbers are a must with Sunday dinner.

3 lb boneless rump roast, (trimmed and tied), or game
6 allspice corns
1/4 tsp. white pepper
1 tsp. salt
approximately 2 cups water
2 tbsp. butter
1 large onion
1 carrot

- Trim away some of the excess fat.
- Salt and pepper the roast.
- Melt the butter in a deep skillet or heavy Dutch oven with a lid. Add the meat and brown a few minutes on each side.
- Add part of the water (cover the bottom of the pan).
- Slice the onions and carrots into thick pieces and add to pan along with the allspice.
- Cover and simmer over low heat, turning and basting roast periodically. Add water regularly so it doesn't boil away.
- Approximate cooking time is 90 minutes.

Gravy

1/2-1 cup water
1 tbsp. flour
1/2 cup cream or whole milk
salt and pepper

- After roast is done and removed from the pan add water to release the pan juices.
- Strain the pan juices into a bowl.
- Stir in the flour with a whisk.
- Dilute with cream or milk or use a bit of both, to taste.
- Season with salt and pepper.

Grandmother's Pickled Pressed Cucumbers

1/2 lb cucumber
2 tbsp. distilled vinegar
2 tbsp. sugar
1/3 cup water
1 tsp. salt
a pinch of white pepper
parsley

- Rinse the cucumbers and slice them thinly.
- Layer cucumber slices in a bowl, sprinkling a little chopped parsley between the layers.
- Whisk together sugar, salt, white pepper, distilled vinegar and water.
- Pour the mixture over the cucumbers.
- Place a weight on top of the cucumbers so they are all covered with the brine.
- Place in the refrigerator for about an hour before serving.

Hasselback Potatoes

This beloved potato dish was created at the Hasselback Restaurant School in Stockholm right after the end of the Second World War. Frugality ruled, so the only option for creativity in the kitchen was to let the imagination run free with the cheap, basic ingredients that were available. Hasselback's newly certified chefs popularized their unique potato dish in restaurants across the land.

2 potatoes per person
butter to brush the potatoes with
dried breadcrumbs
grated cheese

Oven temperature: 425° F

- The secret to Hasselback potatoes is to make sure they stay attached at the base.

Peel each potato and slice thinly without actually cutting all the way through the potato. It can be helpful to set the potato on the counter next to the cutting board, so that the board will prevent the knife from slicing all the way down to the bottom of the potato.

- Butter an ovenproof dish. Place the potatoes in it cut side up.

- Bake about 30 minutes, then remove the dish from the oven, melt a little butter and brush it on the potatoes. Sprinkle breadcrumbs and finely grated cheese on top.
- Put the potatoes back in the oven and let them bake until they have turned golden. Cauliflower, carrots and peas, together with fruit preserves complete the traditional Swedish Sunday dinner.

KING'S MERINGUES

The perfect dessert to end a Sunday dinner is, without doubt, king's meringues with whipped cream and chocolate sauce. Yummy!

Makes about 40 meringues

3 egg whites
3/4 cup sugar

Oven temperature: 275–300° F

- Beat the egg whites until they are so stiff you can turn the bowl upside down without them falling out. Carefully fold in the sugar.
- Scoop egg whites into a sealable plastic bag.
- Snip off the corner of the bag and use the opening as a nib to shape the meringues. Squeeze the egg whites into the desired shapes on a baking sheet prepared with baking parchment. Try to make the meringues roughly the same size so they cook evenly.
- Bake the meringues on the middle rack of the oven for approximately 40 minutes. Just before the meringues are done open the oven door slightly to make meringues dry and light.

Chocolate Sauce

3/4 cup water
5 tbsp. cocoa
1/2 cup sugar

1 1/4 cups heavy cream for whipping

- Combine the water, cocoa, and sugar in a saucepan. Let the sauce simmer over low heat until it thickens to a desired consistency.
- Let it cool.
- Whip the cream.
- Arrange the meringues on a large platter. Place a layer of whipped cream on top. Drizzle the chocolate sauce over the whipped cream using a spoon or a thin straw.

Exams and End of School Year

In Sweden, compulsory school ends after the ninth grade. But then there is no graduation celebration with caps and gowns. You receive your graduation cap first after two to four years studies at "Gymnasium", (similar to something between High School and College). The cap is white with black brims and a blue and yellow emblem. The colors on the velvet band around the cap vary according to the subject one chose for his or her program. The "Gymnasium" graduation ritual in Sweden is called "Studentexamen". For a number of years during the seventies and eighties it wasn't especially acceptable to celebrate passing of the exam; everything that had to do with such ancient traditions was to be sabotaged. As a child I loved the custom of passing the "Studentexamen" and looked forward to passing it myself. The celebration of exams

and weddings were my favourite ceremonial occasions.

When I grew up there also existed another graduation ritual called "Real Examen". At that time the compulsory school ended with the seventh grade and if you continued two more years at "Realen" and passed the final test, you'd receive the same cap with the only exception that it was grey. In those days, you didn't know if you would receive your degree until you had passed the final examination, which was given a few hours before the ceremony. The pressure was on for the poor students, who knew their families were gathered outside the schoolyard with congratulatory placards, waiting to take them to receptions with relatives.

Flowers, small teddy bears and other stuffed animals with miniature student caps were

hung around the necks of the happy graduates, who toured the town making champagne toasts on floats decorated with greenery. I was always very happy when a graduated relative gave me a mini-cap. I used the mini-caps for my Barbie dolls, who were constantly graduating from high school themselves. We also had cool little plastic mini-caps that were used to decorate cakes. I'll never forget the disappointment when my uncle graduated and we opened the cake to find that the baker had made the caps out of marzipan. I could only say "Ew!".

When it was time for me to graduate, the "Real Examen" had long been done away with and the gray caps were just a memory. Instead, you had to wait two, three or four years to take the "Studentexamen". I believe I was the only one in my class to buy a student cap. If I remember right, I never put it on at graduation, because I probably would have been booed. But I still wanted to have one, not least because of all the memories of how much I'd loved them as a child. Today, graduation has reclaimed its place and is more popular than ever. Parties are numerous, the celebrations are large, and it's expected that one will wear the white cap.

In Sweden it's not only graduation that counts; everyone celebrates the end of the school year! These celebrations are often held in church; in some places they are held in the school auditorium. It is almost obligatory to sing "The Time of Flowers Is Now Here", a summer hymn that gives most people goose bumps when they hear the first few notes. Nothing is more closely associated with summer and free time than that song. Occasionally, however, a song will come along to challenge "The Time of Flowers'" popularity. One such tune is "Ida's Summer Song", from the film about Emil in Lönneberga written by Astrid Lindgren.

The end of the school year also brings to mind the scent of lilac blossoms. Every year, I received a giant bouquet from my grandparents from the white lilac bush in their garden. Around our house on Gotland, purple lilac bushes bloom in the beginning of June; they give off a wonderful scent. And before the lilacs, the bird-cherries bloom. There are some who claim that summer is most beautiful just in between the blooming of the bird-cherries and the lilacs, which happens early in June when the summer nights are short and the light is fantastic. Ulf Lundell, who has been named the Swedish national bard, both writes and sings about the magic of the time between the blooming of the bird-cherries and the lilac.

Mother's Day is celebrated in Sweden on the last Sunday in May, a custom modeled on the American holiday, which was celebrated for the first time in 1919. In school, we would draw pictures for our mothers, and when I was old enough to use the oven by myself I would bake a cake for my mother.

Ascension Day is usually celebrated before the end of the school year. Like Easter, it is a movable holiday that occurs forty days after Easter Sunday. It always falls on a Thursday, which means that the majority of Swedes take the opportunity to take off Friday for an extra day of free time. Ascension Day is known as a big fishing day, since many take the opportunity to try their luck fishing. Other popular activities are working in the garden or having a picnic. It used to be common to take the picnic basket and go out to listen to the first cuckoo, commonly called "the dawn cuckoo". Young people used to amuse themselves on Ascension Day by taking walks to neighboring parishes to listen to the sermons in other churches, but the main object was probably to meet the youth of other parishes along the way, which from time to time resulted in an engagement.

National Day

▸ Since 1983, June 6 has been Sweden's National Day. It took a long time for Sweden to declare a National Day, though June 6 had long been celebrated as Swedish Flag Day. Since the turn of the century Swedes had been discussing an appropriate day on which to celebrate the Swedish nation. In 1916 it was decided that Sweden would celebrate Swedish Flag Day on June 6th until the question of a national day was resolved. June 6th was also known as Gustav Day, in memory of Gustav Vasa, who was crowned King of Sweden on June 6, 1523. On the same day in 1809, Sweden adopted a new Constitution.

Artur Hazelius was the founder of the big open-air museum Skansen in 1893, a huge national festival. But since it had been almost completely rained out, he decided to hold the festival again on Gustav Day, June 6. This quickly became a tradition, a day when school children and adults carried flags on a pilgrimage to Skansen. The Swedish Flag was not officially adopted by the country until 1906. When the Swedish flag was first raised over the royal palace in 1873, there were many who thought that a flag had no place on land and was better suited to sea-going vessels. But it didn't take long for flagpoles to become popular additions to schoolyards, train stations and other places. In 1916, the Swedish Flag Day was celebrated with pomp and ceremony in Stockholm's shiny new stadium, recently completed for the 1912 Summer Olympics. King Gustav V and other members of the royal family attended.

The tradition of celebrating Swedish Flag Day in Stockholm Stadium continued until 1963 when people decided to move the celebration to Skansen. Twenty years later Flag Day was transformed into Sweden's National Day. On the inaugural National Day, Queen Silvia wore the Swedish national costume, which she had commissioned for herself and the two princesses especially for the occasion. But we still have a long way to go before it becomes as much of a holiday as the national day of Norway, our neighbor to the west. There, May 17 is the big day and all of Karl Johan Street is filled with flag-waving Norwegians. But it is a festive feeling, of course, to be at Skansen and see the royal family arrive by horse and carriage, listen to the Swedish National anthem, and see the many proud Swedes waving their blue and yellow flags.

COD WITH EGG SAUCE

Cod was once one of the most popular fish in Swedish cooking. Unfortunately it is now considered something of a delicacy because of overfishing.

Classic cod with egg sauce was one of my favorite dishes when I was a child. I remember how I used to run to the store to buy frozen cod, which came in blocks. I think I was quite old before I understood what a codfish really looked like.

1 1/2 lb cod filets
3 quarts water for boiling
6 tsp. salt
6 black peppercorns

For the egg sauce:

1 oz butter
1/2 cup fish stock
2-3 eggs
1/2 tsp. salt

- Hard boil eggs.
- Add salt and peppercorns to three quarts of water, bring to a boil.

- Carefully add the cod filets to the boiling water.
- Reduce heat and simmer, covered, for 5 -10 minutes or until fish flakes easily with fork. Reserve stock.
- Mash the eggs.
- Melt the butter in a saucepan and add 1/2 cup of fish stock (take stock from the boiling fish) and mashed egg. Let it cook for a couple of minutes.
- Serve with boiled potatoes.

BEEF RYDBERG

This is a high end variation on Swedish hash from the Hotel Rydberg in Stockholm, which used to be located on Gustav Adolfs Torg. Now the hotel is only a memory, but Beef Rydberg lives on in most restaurants in Stockholm. There are a number of recipes for Beef Rydberg, but all versions are served with raw egg yolks and mustard. We like to eat it with a little freshly grated horseradish.

1 lb filet of beef
1 large yellow onion
6 medium potatoes
Worcestershire sauce
butter or margarine for sautéing
salt and white pepper

Serve with raw egg yolks, mustard and fresh horseradish, if desired. Canned horseradish also works well.

- Peel potatoes and optional dice them into small cubes.
- Cut the beef into small, rectangular pieces.
- Finely chop the onion.
- Sauté the diced potatoes over low to medium heat until they are soft all the way through. Add the onion toward the end.
- Cover potatoes to keep warm and set aside.
- Sear the meat over high heat to quickly brown the outside, keeping the inside pink. Add some Worcestershire sauce to taste.
- Reserve the pan juices to pour over the meat.

POTATO CAKES

Potato cakes are my husband's absolute favorite food. He is hardly off the plane in Stockholm before he rushes to his favorite restaurant, PA & Co, to eat potato cakes.

8 medium potatoes

butter or margarine for frying

For serving:

6 oz fish roe of choice (red caviar)
2 chopped red onions
1 cup sour cream
dill
lemon

- Grate the potatoes on the coarsest side of the grater.
- Add a good-sized pat of butter or margarine in a frying pan.

- With your hands, form a ball of grated potatoes the size of a golf ball. Place it in the frying pan and flatten with a spatula.
- Fry the potato cakes over medium high heat, approximately 3 minutes on each side until golden brown.
- Serve immediately with sour cream, fish roe, red onion, lemon and fresh dill.

SAUTÉED SALMON WITH SPINACH

Sautéed salmon with spinach was my grandfather's specialty and inseparable from my memories of summer and his country house in Tylösand on the Swedish west coast.

Back then salmon was considered a luxury as it was difficult to come by. Today the practice of salmon farming and cleaner waters for wild salmon mean that everyone can enjoy this tasty fish.

Serves 4

4 salmon steaks, approximately 1/2 inch thick
1 tsp. salt
black pepper
1 lemon
butter for cooking

- Scrape off the fish scales. Dry off and salt the salmon steaks.
- Melt the butter in the frying pan.
- Cook the salmon steaks over medium heat, 3-4 minutes per side.
- Sprinkle the salmon with pepper and a few drops of lemon.
- Serve with boiled potatoes and spinach.

Spinach

1 lb spinach, preferably fresh
4 cups water
2 tsp. salt
black pepper
lemon

- Bring the water to a boil.
- Place the freshly washed spinach in the boiling water.
- Let it boil 3-4 minutes. Drain.
- Season the spinach with salt, pepper and lemon before serving.

MILDLY CURED LAX WITH POTATOES AND DILL SAUCE

Mildly cured lax is similar to gravlax, except for the proportion of salt and sugar. The combination of mildly cured lax and dill potatoes is a true classic, offering many Swedish taste experiences on the same plate.

Mildly Cured Lax

3 lb salmon, center cut from a large salmon
6 tbsp. salt
4 tbsp. sugar

- It is best to leave the salmon in the freezer for five days to kill off any parasites.
- Remove the spine and all other visible bones. A pair of tongs or tweezers is usually helpful.
- Combine the sugar and salt in a bowl.
- Thoroughly rub the sugar and salt mixture into each piece of salmon.
- Lay one piece of the salmon skin side down on a large piece of plastic wrap.
- Place the other piece of fish on top, skin side up.
- Cover them with the plastic wrap.
- Place in the refrigerator.
- After 12 hours pour off any accumulated excess liquid.
- Let it sit 1-2 days in the refrigerator before serving.

Potatoes in Dill Sauce

8 medium potatoes
1 1/2 cups whole milk
2 tbsp. flour
2 tbsp. butter or margarine
1/2 tsp. salt
a pinch of white pepper
dill

- Peel the potatoes and cut them into cubes.
- Rinse them before cooking.
- Boil them in enough water to cover them. Add a little salt to the water.
- When the potatoes are almost done, pour off the water.
- Using another saucepan. Melt the butter or margarine, add the flour and mix it together. Pour 1/2 cup of milk and stir immediately and then add more milk until the mixture thickens.
- Carefully stir the potatoes into the mixture.
- Add salt, pepper and freshly chopped dill as desired.

WEST COAST SALAD

I remember it as if it were yesterday: Friday evening with west coast salad and toast in front of the TV. Salads were not as common when I grew up in the 70s as they are now, so this was a rather festive meal at the time.

3 tomatoes
2 hard-boiled eggs cut in wedges
8 oz mushrooms
1 small head iceberg lettuce
1/2 cucumber
8 oz cooked, peeled shrimp
10-15 (blue) mussels or one can mussels
1 can white asparagus or one bunch fresh asparagus
3/4 cup frozen green peas
1 lemon

- Begin by cooking the shrimp and the mussels if they are raw.
- Hard boil eggs.
- Thaw frozen peas.
- Cut the tomatoes and eggs into wedges.
- Slice the mushrooms, cucumber and lemon.
- Peel the shrimp.

- Cut the asparagus in thirds.
- Combine everything in a large salad bowl.
- Tear the iceberg lettuce into good-sized pieces and mix them into the salad.
- Finally, garnish with the mussels, letting them remain in their shells.
- If you wish, you can add lobster to the salad for even more delicious flavor.

Rhode Island Sauce

1/2 cup mayonnaise
1/2 cup sour cream
2 tbsp. chili sauce

- Blend all the ingredients together in a dish.
- Season, if desired, with salt and pepper.

Whitsuntide – a Big Holiday for Weddings

Whitsuntide falls fifty days after Easter, some time between May 10 and June 13, and has become a popular time for weddings.

Even in earlier times young people used to have parties, especially on the second day of Whitsuntide. Food, drink, and money were scraped together by begging throughout the countryside. They would choose a Whitsun bride who would be dressed up and decorated with flowers. Sometimes the most beautiful girl in the area was chosen, but she wasn't always willing to do it; being a Whitsun bride could garner one a bad reputation, since all the boys in the area would get to dance with her. Instead, the bride was often a poor girl who was paid to play the part.

In farming communities the weather at Whitsuntide was of great importance because it was said to have an effect on the harvest. Rain, for example, might be taken as prediction that the crops would be ruined. Animals were given rowan branches to chew on, and those who took care of the animals were supposed to eat eggs in the barn—all for extra luck and success during the summer.

Now it's more the bridal couple that worries about the weather, even though it's said to bring luck if the bride gets rain on her bridal crown. Once upon a time, people didn't choose their husband or wife for love; instead it was something that the parents decided when the

children were little. The proposal was made later according to predetermined customs. When all concerned parties had come to an agreement, the engagement happened when the husband- and wife-to-be exchanged presents. Then the banns were read in the church. If it was a large wedding the festivities could go on for a week. Often the wedding was held in the bride's home. It was typical for the wedding to take place between Christmas and New Year's, for that was when the pantries were full of food and people had free time. Easter, Whitsuntide, and Midsummer were also popular holidays for weddings. In earlier times, the bride was dressed not in white but in black, later with a white veil. The bridal gown was intended to serve as a good dress for the bride's whole life. The bride's most distinctive adornment was the crown, which she could borrow from the church. If you want to have a Whitsun wedding today, it is best to book the church far in advance, as well as the priest.

Swedish weddings differ appreciably from American ones, not least when it comes to the number of wedding guests, which seldom matches up to a wedding in the U.S. The planning is usually not as involved, either. Many choose to have the wedding in their home church; in Sweden people have the right to wed in their home church free of charge. The extent of food and drink varies. Some choose to have the dinner at a restaurant, with all the service included, others hire caterers and set up in a rented hall. There are also those who choose to prepare the food themselves to keep costs down, allowing them to invite more guests.

This last variation was the one my husband and I chose when we had our wedding some years ago. It was a day that left us wonderful memories without leaving us flat broke. We chose to get married on Gotland, Sweden's largest island, where we have our summer house. We simply rented an old school for the weekend. The school had been turned into a youth hostel, which meant that there was lodging for quite a few of the overnight guests, as well as a common room large enough to hold a hundred wedding guests. The food was a homemade buffet that I was mostly responsible for, and the cakes were summery strawberry cakes.

The marriage trend seems to fluctuate a lot in Sweden. There are still many who choose to just live together, and since the laws changed there is almost no legal difference between being married and living together. For many a wedding is more of a chance to throw a big party and gather family and friends together. One does sometimes see bridal couples who have been inspired by American weddings, who devote a great deal of time and energy to making everything perfect. As for myself, I have to admit that our wedding was planned well enough to leave lots of room for spontaneity, which felt wonderful.

When I was little I loved weddings. Most of all I wanted to be a bridesmaid, and I was, three times. I really liked that little mini-bridal bouquet. For my own wedding, I picked my own Gotland bridal bouquet from the wildflowers in the meadow one hour before the wedding, dressed in rubber boots and shorts. When some of my guests caught sight of me and my daughter, who was picking her bridesmaid bouquet, they looked horrified: isn't today the wedding? Oh, yes, we're going to go home and change. My girlfriend, Gisela, made my dress in a turn-of-the-century style. That's what happened to all the lace in the family! But it would surely have languished in some forgotten box or drawer otherwise.

Believe it or not, we made it to the church just in time to walk down the aisle. My husband and daughter were responsible for one of the most unforgettable moments of the entire wedding. In my foolishness, I believed I could avoid all that wedding waltz stuff. And in a way I did, but there *was* a dance—when the music started and Pet Shop Boys' "New York City Boy" came blasting out of the loudspeakers no one was more surprised than the bride herself. What a success!

Midsummer and Finally Summer is Here

▶▶ Just like Swedish Christmas, Midsummer is widely celebrated and recognized the world over. Many believe it is the most Swedish holiday of all. The true Midsummer Day falls on June 24. In 1953, however, they decided to move the celebrations to the Saturday between June 20 and June 26. Just like Christmas, Easter, Walpurgis Eve, and Pentecost, the eve of the actual holiday is the big day to celebrate on. Thus, Friday is the day people dance around the midsummer pole, or Maypole. In many places, people have made the actual setting up of the Maypole, or "maying", into its own ceremony during which the whole village gathers to decorate the pole with birch twigs and flowers. Two flower wreaths are hung on the pole, which is formed like a cross. There is no proof that the Midsummer pole acts as a fertility charm, but there is a saying to the effect that Midsummer night may not be long but it sets seventy-seven cradles a-rocking.

In Dalarna, where, according to many people, they celebrate Midsummer to the fullest, the pole looks a little different, and they also leave the pole standing after the festival. Stationary poles of this type from the sixteen and seventeen hundreds have been found in Västergötland, Östergötland and Skåne. If you look back in history, you will find that the Maypole has its origin in Germany in the 1400s, where they decorated Maypoles with leaves in May. At that time of year, Sweden has relatively few leaves, so Swedes decided to decorate their poles in Midsummer instead. Large leaf markets were held in Stockholm in the square at Munkbrotorget, then later at Riddarholmskanalen, on June 22 and 23. Decorating with flowers and leaves was so popular that a forest ordinance was enacted in 1784, forbidding people to cover large rooms and churches with the leafy branches of young birch trees, which were being depleted. The lea-

ves of the rowan tree could not be left out or forgotten, however, as they were believed to bring good luck. Many Midsummer poles were sold at the leaf markets the way we sell Christmas trees for Christmas today. There were all types, clad in everything from paper, gauze, ribbons, and taffeta to gold paper, egg-shells, and streamers.

Besides the Midsummer poles, most of the manors and farms of Gotland had spars that were stored in the churches. People were allo-wed to decorate these for Midsummer and carry them in a musical procession into the churches.

The superstition surrounding the shortest night of the year is great. In the past, healing herbs were picked during Midsummer night because they were believed to have greater power then than on other days. It was said the most efficacious method for gathering the her-bs was to walk into the meadow or church-yard backwards and pick the herbs with your left hand. The herbs were then dried, and often added to aquavit, which was considered an excellent healing tonic, especially in combi-nation with these healing herbs. Even dew was considered more valuable when collected on

Midsummer night, so people laid out their bed sheets to absorb the dew, and sometimes even rolled naked in the dew. Farmers would keep watch on Midsummer night so no uninvited neighbors would try to steal their dew. Dew thieves might wring out the stolen sheets over their own land, thereby ensuring their own good crops and fat animals at the expense of the farmer whose dew they stole—in fact, everything would be worse for him!

Ferns were thought to bloom once a year. If a man managed to snatch such a fern blooming on Midsummer night, he was guaranteed good luck with women for the rest of his life.

Even today, girls pick seven or sometimes nine different kinds of flowers (the number varies from region to region) and place under the pillow before they fall asleep. That night, in their dreams, they will see the man they are going to share their life with. According to tradition, the flowers are picked in silence, after which the girl must climb over seven (or nine) fences. A peek into the future can also be achieved by throwing a coin into a spring, which then reflects the future in its waters. Drinking the water from the spring is considered both good luck and good for your health.

Musicians with violins and accordions, folk-dress and folk-dancers are all part of Midsummer celebrations. The most traditional dance of all is probably the ring dance. That's when all the old joyous songs, which are also sung during the dance around the Christmas tree, are performed. Big and little, young and

old, do not hesitate to dance like frogs, musicians, bears, or other things. To an observer who doesn't know about these traditions it can seem a little strange. If you've grown up with it, it seems the most natural thing in the world.

Girls large and small wear a wreath of flowers in their hair. There are many variations; some are made with wildflowers from the meadow while others are elegant wreaths bound with great care and precision. From the time I was a year old, all my wreaths were made of cornflowers and daisies, and I couldn't imagine a Midsummer wreath any other way. That's why my daughter's has always looked the same. When she was little she wanted her belo-

ved stuffed Mickey Mouse to have a wreath, and who could say no to that? Fashioning a Midsummer wreath demands patience; usually more than one flower falls off before you are done, which means you have to begin all over again. Binding a wreath of Midsummer flowers is nothing new; people have done it since time immemorial. It was once considered wise to save the wreath. If you fell ill, you could burn the wreath, as the smoke it gave off was considered healing. If you hadn't burned the wreath before Christmas, you could place it in the bath water for your Christmas bath to make it extra strengthening.

Ironically, Midsummer weather is never what one would wish. Rain, gray, and cold are more a Midsummer memory than blue sky and sun; one might certainly wonder if Midsummer is statistically guaranteed to be the year's rainiest day. My husband is stubborn, however, and we have to sit outside regardless of the weather and eat herring and new potatoes and drink schnapps, with strawberries and whipped cream for dessert, a menu that I know we share with most Swedes that day. My daughter and I sit outside with floral wreaths in our hair, shivering in our nice summer dresses, wrapped in blankets and happy we have schnapps to warm us. After the Midsummer meal it's time to ride our bikes along the paths through the woods to the dancing. Everyone in the neighborhood makes their way to the grounds of a fine, old, traditional manor house to decorate the Midsummer pole and dance

around it. All the children are usually served ice cream, and grownups can buy cinnamon buns and coffee if they haven't brought along their own picnic basket.

For my family, Midsummer is inseparable from Gotland, but last year, I chose to celebrate Midsummer on American soil, since I'd heard so many wonderful things about it; quite simply, I was curious. Midsummer celebrations in Battery Park in New York City are not so different from the Swedish ones, especially as the raindrops were hanging threateningly overhead the whole time. It was powerful to watch all the wreath-bedecked people eating

hotdogs in the park, and turn to see the Statue of Liberty in one direction and the mighty skyscrapers of Lower Manhattan in the other. There was, of course, that enormous empty space, which saddened us all on that festive day.

I spent my childhood Midsummers on the west coast of Sweden in Tylösand, outside Halmstad. There were tons of children there. In addition to the obligatory herring, poached salmon was usually on the menu, served later in the evening. After the dancing I was finally permitted to take the year's first dip in the sea, and it didn't matter whether it was freezing cold or not. We had to go in at any cost. I was a

real little fish as a child; I loved to spend the most time possible in the water and managed to bring home many swimming badges. Some years it was exceedingly cold when swimming school began, but that didn't stop me. I remember when my swimming coaches stood on the dock and shivered while I struggled with my two thousand meter breaststroke. After fifteen hundred meters, they said let's call it two thousand meters now. No, I said stubbornly, I have five hundred meters left. The poor swimming coaches just shook their heads. Probably my lips were blue and they were deathly afraid I would get a cramp. Luckily, I finished the two thousand meters without incident.

The most wonderful thing about the Swedish summer is the light; seeing the sun go down around 11 p.m., rising again at 2:30 a.m. One comes to appreciate how truly dependent people are on light for their survival; with all the extra sunlight, people suddenly don't need all those extra hours of sleep to have the energy to stay awake. If it's a good summer, which is never guaranteed, the Swedish summer is probably among the most beautiful there is. I understand how tourists who come to Stockholm on a summer day think the city is com-

pletely enchanting. It is lovely in other ways as well, but I have to admit after twenty years there that the city looks better bathed in sunshine than beneath rain-laden skies.

All of Sweden is beautiful, especially in the summer. Gotland, as I've said, is the place where we have chosen to spend our summers. If you look at the statistics, there are more sunny days there than in other parts of Sweden, but that wasn't the main reason we chose to settle there. It was more that we fell in love with the island and everything it had to offer. To come directly from the clamor of New York to the silence on Gotland is an amazing change. Gotland is so quiet; you almost can't sleep the first few days. Then you get used to it, and the rhythm of country life soon feels normal. We don't venture out much farther than a few kilometers. There are trips to the fisherman in Lergrav where we buy fresh fish, and to the greengrocer in Lärbro where we buy fruit and vegetables, and then the big decision is whether to go to the thriving metropolis of Slite, with a gigantic quarry as its main tourist attraction, or Fårösund, where you sometimes bump into Ingmar Bergman in the grocery store. For the most part, we stay at home and devote our days to small tasks and swimming, and in the evening we grill outdoors, with my husband in charge of the grill, and enjoy the view of the sunset. It has a certain kind of beauty that there are no words for. It is, naturally, wonderful for our daughter to be able to bicycle, pick flowers, swim, and thread wild strawberries onto a piece of straw. I enjoy seeing how her summers are full of exactly what a child's summer vacation should be full of: life and pleasure.

Of my own summer vacations, what I remember most is that I earned money. There was always something at the top of my wish list that I wanted, so I would try to work hard enough to get it. When I was growing up, there were lots of summer jobs for children and young adults. I usually spent my summers gluing on labels at Grandfather's factory. It was piecework so it was important to really apply yourself if you wanted to earn anything. A little later, I used to pick strawberries at my Grandfather's brother's farm, just like all the other children in the village. We got five cents per liter and a sunburn on our backs. One year, by the time summer vacation was over, I had managed to save enough money to buy my first real SLR camera. That laid the foundation for what would one day be my profession, a profession that has allowed me to travel the world, meeting celebrities and royals and the like. One royal I met was the Swedish crown princess Victoria. Her birthday falls in the middle of the summer, July 14, a day many wish to celebrate in her honor. The crown princess receives the birthday greetings of her people at the royal summer residence, Solliden, on Öland. Afterward, the festivities continue at Borgholm's sports arena, featuring some of the greatest artists of the year. Who doesn't want to be a part of it and sing for the crown prin-

cess? Through my job, I've had the chance to take part and celebrate the crown princess's birthday, and it's a special moment when the King gives the command to sing "Happy Birthday" and the whole audience joins in.

A few days after the crown princess's birthday, it's time to eat cake almost every day, for that is when Ladies Week occurs. Ladies Week begins with Sara on July 19, and continues with Margareta, Johanna, Magdalena, Emma, and Kristina. Jakob or Fredrik, which are men's names, gets tacked on to make it a complete week. All women whose names are mentioned above are fêted because their Name Day falls during that week. In Sweden, we celebrate everyone's Name Day, which is like an extra mini-birthday. But you don't have to know anybody named Sara, Margareta, Johanna, Magdalena, Emma, Kristina or Jakob to participate in the Ladies Week festivities. Just ask my husband; he looks for any opportunity to celebrate with a cake!

PICKLED HERRING

"Silver of the sea"—that was what herring was called in earlier times when it was everyday food. These days it is a delicacy mainly eaten at Christmas, Easter and Midsummer. Herring is also superb washed down with a shot of schnapps.

  16 oz herring in wine sauce
  1 cup water
  1/2 cup 5% distilled vinegar
  1/2 cup sugar
  2 red onions
  1 carrot
  2 bay leaves
  10 allspice corns, crushed
  5 whole cloves

- Bring the water, vinegar and sugar to a boil. Add the bay leaves and spices.
- Heat until the sugar has melted.
- Remove from the heat and let cool.
- Remove herring from the can or jar and rinse gently under cold, running water.
- Split the red onion in two and cut the halves into semicircular slices.
- Peel and slice the carrot.
- In a glass jar, alternate layers of herring with layers of carrot and red onion.
- Add the cooled brine to the jar.
- It tastes best if left to stand in the refrigerator for at least one day before serving.

Fish Roe Herring

6 oz Matjes herring
1/2 cup sour cream
1/3 cup mayonnaise
1/2 medium red onion
1 tbsp. red caviar

- Finely chop the onion.
- Blend the mayonnaise and sour cream.
- Add the onion.
- Add the Matjes herring and stir so that it is well blended.
- Carefully stir in the caviar.

Tomato Herring

8 oz herring in wine sauce
4 tbsp. red vinegar
3 tbsp. cooking oil
6 tbsp. tomato puree
6 tbsp. sugar
4 tbsp. water
1 small onion
10 allspice corns, crushed
a pinch of white pepper

- Rinse the herring gently under cold, running water.
- Transfer to a glass jar.
- Finely chop the onion and add to jar.
- Mix vinegar, oil, tomato puree, sugar and spices with the water.
- Pour the mixture over the herring and, if possible, leave to stand in the refrigerator for an hour or so before serving.

Horseradish Herring

6 oz Matjes herring
1/2 cup sour cream
1/3 cup mayonnaise
2 tsp. mustard, preferably whole grain honey mustard
grated horseradish as desired

- Combine all ingredients in a bowl.
- Transfer mixture to a glass jar and let stand in the refrigerator a few hours before serving.

Herring à la Russe

6 oz Matjes herring, preferably whole filets
1/2 cup mayonnaise
1/2 cup sour cream
1 tsp. mustard

1-2 chopped hard-boiled eggs
4 tbsp. pickled beets (see recipe p. 30)
4 tbsp. pickled cucumbers
1 tbsp. capers
1 tbsp. chopped chives

- Place the herring on a plate. (If you use whole filets, cut them into smaller pieces first.)
- Combine mayo, sour cream and mustard. Pour over herring.
- Garnish with beets, pickled cucumbers, capers, eggs and chives.

MATJES HERRING TORTE

This is a perfect appetizer that usually impresses everyone.

10 oz pumpernickel bread
4 oz butter
6 oz Matjes herring (reserve 2 tbsp. brine)
one bunch chives
1 cup sour cream or crème fraiche
1 cup creamed, whipped cottage cheese
2 tbsp. brine from the Matjes herring
2 oz red caviar
2 oz black caviar

- Pulse bread in a food processor until it turns to crumbs.
- Melt butter and pour over the breadcrumbs. Mix to form a dough.
- Cover the bottom of a 10-inch pie pan (with a removable bottom) with plastic wrap. Line the bottom with the breadcrumb mixture. Pat it down with a fork and place pan in the freezer for 1-2 hours.
- Turn the breadcrumb crust out of the pan onto a serving plate. Remove the plastic wrap.
- Chop herring. Chop chives (save a few chopped chives for garnish) and combine in a dish. Pour reserved brine over mixture.
- Blend sour cream or crème fraiche with cottage cheese and add into the herring mix.
- Spread the mixture on the bread crumb base. Garnish with red and black caviar and chives.

SCHNAPPS

In earlier times alcohol was seen as a fortifying drink, not an intoxicant. For this reason, spirits were taken often and in overly large doses. Alcohol helped to alleviate the cold, melancholy and the darkness. Up until the middle of the 1700s almost all alcohol was made from grain. Then one day Eva de la Gardie, the first woman member of the Academy of Science, discovered that you could use potatoes to make schnapps, saving valuable seed for food in the process.

But the bad taste of fusel oil—the acrid byproduct of incompletely distilled alcohol—made the alcohol taste repellent. To cover up the bad taste people flavored the schnapps with spices from various plants. It wasn't until the end of the 1800s that the schnapps king, L.O. Smith, managed to distill a schnapps that was absolutely pure. It is his portrait we see on the Absolut Vodka bottle.

L.O. Smith's discovery has not prevented us from continuing to flavor alcohol. So let your imagination run wild and try flavoring your own schnapps. One note: berry flavored schnapps only keeps for a limited time.

Don't forget to sing when you take a drink—the schnapps goes down better! Or at least let out a "Skål!," in remembrance of the time when they still drank schnapps out of skulls.

Berry Schnapps

1/2 cup vodka, or enough to cover
the berries
1 cup berries – raspberries, blackberries, blueberries or plums

- Mix berries and vodka. Let the mixture steep one week in the fridge and then strain out berries.
- Add more vodka according to taste. One cup is suggested.

Vanilla Schnapps

1 vanilla bean
1/2 cup vodka

- Cover the vanilla bean with the vodka. Keep it in a jar with the lid on for a month.
- Add more vodka according to taste. One cup is suggested. Let the vanilla bean stay in one more week, then remove it.

Aniseed, Fennel and Caraway Schnapps

1 tsp. aniseed
1 tsp. fennel seeds
1 tsp. caraway
12 oz vodka

- Put the spices in a glass, add 4 oz vodka and let stand 12 hours.

- Strain with a tea strainer.
- Add 8 oz vodka, transfer to a bottle and let stand a few days.

Lemon Balm Schnapps

40 lemon balm leaves
12 oz vodka

- Place the lemon balm leaves in a glass and pour 4 oz vodka over them.
- Cover the glass with plastic wrap. Let stand about a week.
- Strain out the leaves and pour the liquid into a bottle.
- Add 8 oz vodka, or more, to taste.

Dill and Coriander Schnapps

1/4 cup fresh dill
1/2 tsp. whole coriander (40 corns)
12 oz vodka

- Crush coriander with a mortar and pestle.
- Mix the dill and crushed coriander in a glass. Add 4 oz vodka. Let stand twelve hours.
- Strain with a tea strainer.
- Add 8 oz vodka, transfer to a bottle and let stand for a week.

POACHED SALMON

A whole poached salmon is a great entree to serve when you have many people gathered round the dining room table. If you want a cold sauce with it, sharp sauce makes the perfect accompaniment. If you prefer a warm sauce, white wine sauce or hollandaise sauce are excellent choices.

Serves 12

7 lb salmon
5 quarts water
10 tsp. salt
2 carrots
1 yellow onion

- Rinse off the salmon.
- Place it in a fish poacher.
- Fill with water until the salmon is covered. Add salt, 1 tsp. for every pint of water.
- Peel carrots and cut them into large chunks. Quarter a peeled onion and add to poaching pan with carrots.
- Bring the water to a boil then let the fish simmer over low heat for about 30-40 minutes.

Sharp Sauce

1 hard-boiled egg
1 raw egg yolk
1/2 tsp. salt
a pinch of white pepper
1 tsp. French mustard, preferably 1/2 tsp. seeded and 1/2 tsp. seedless
1 tbsp. white wine vinegar
1 tbsp. capers
a pinch of sugar
2/3 cup heavy cream, whipped
dill

- Remove yolk from hard-boiled egg.
- Mash the boiled egg yolk in a bowl and mix with raw egg yolk.
- Mince capers and mix with vinegar, mustard, salt, sugar and white pepper. Add to egg yolks.
- Mix in the whipped cream.
- Add desired amount chopped dill.

Hollandaise Sauce

3 tbsp. butter or margarine
2 tbsp. all-purpose flour
3/4 cup fish stock, (cube of fish bouillon dissolved in water, for example)
2 egg yolks
1/2 cup heavy cream
2 tbsp. fresh lemon juice
salt and white pepper
cayenne pepper

- Melt the butter in a saucepan.
- Stir the flour into the butter and add a little fish stock at a time to form a thick sauce, stirring constantly.

- Combine the egg yolks with the cream and add to pan when the sauce begins to thicken. Let the sauce simmer until it reaches desired consistency.
- Season to taste with lemon juice, salt, white pepper and a knife tip of cayenne pepper.

White Wine Sauce

1 1/2 cup fish stock
1/2 cup heavy cream
1/2 cup white wine
1 tbsp. flour
1 tbsp. butter
salt and pepper

- Reduce the fish stock by half by letting it cook at a heavy boil.
- Melt the butter in another saucepan. Stir the flour into the butter and add a little fish stock at a time to form a thick sauce, stirring constantly.
- Add the wine when the sauce begins to thicken and then add the cream. Let the sauce cook until it reaches desired consistency.
- Season with salt and pepper.

POTATO PANCAKES

This is a more substantial version of pancakes with much of the batter composed of finely grated potatoes. Here, however, neither raspberries nor strawberries are served. It is the priceless Swedish lingonberries that go with potato pancakes.

    2 lb potatoes
    3/4 cup all-purpose flour
    1 egg
    2 cups whole milk
    1 tsp. salt
    butter or margarine for frying

- Beat the egg, flour, salt and half the milk into a batter.
- Peel the potatoes. Finely grate them with a hand grater or the grating blade on a food processor.
- Stir the grated potatoes directly to the batter.
- Stir in the rest of the milk.
- Add desire amount for one pancake to a buttered pan and fry golden brown on both sides.
- Serve with lingonberry preserves and bacon.

COD WITH HORSERADISH

The combination of freshly cooked cod with melted butter and freshly grated horseradish is probably among the best things to come out of the Swedish kitchen. We say this every time the dish is brought to the dining room table. If you don't feel like eating cod, pike works just as well, or why not try the delicacy turbot?

1 1/2 lb cod, preferably sliced, otherwise filleted
3 quarts water
6 tsp. salt
6 black peppercorns

4 oz butter for melting
horseradish, preferably a fresh piece to grate, otherwise from a jar
boiled potatoes for serving

- Begin with peeling the potatoes and boiling them.
- Cook the fish in the salted water together with the whole peppercorns. Let it boil for 7-10 minutes.
- If you have fresh horseradish, peel and grate it just before serving, otherwise it can quickly turn green.
- Melt the butter just before the fish is placed on the serving plate.
- Serve fillet drizzled with butter and topped with horseradish and boiled potatoes.

GOTLAND SAFFRON PANCAKE

A Gotland specialty served anytime, from Christmas to Midsummer. There are many recipes from this island, Sweden's largest.

1/2 cup Japanese rice
1 cup water
1/4 tsp. salt
2 cups whole milk
1/2 cup heavy cream
2 tbsp. sugar
0.5 gram saffron
4 eggs
2 oz blanched almonds (approx. 40 almonds)

Oven temperature: 425° F

- Boil the rice with the water and salt in a covered saucepan until the water is absorbed.
- Add the milk and cream and let the rice mixture simmer over a low heat until soft, about 30-40 minutes. Stir from time to time so it doesn't scorch on the bottom. Add a little extra milk if needed.
- Let the mixture cool a little. Stir in the sugar and the saffron.
- Turn on the oven.
- Blanche and peel, if necessary, and chop the almonds.
- Add the eggs to the rice, one at a time. Then add the almonds.
- Pour the rice mixture into a buttered oven-proof dish.
- Bake on the lowest rack of the oven approximately 30 minutes.
- Serve the saffron pancake lightly cooled, with whipped cream and blackberry jam.

BALTIC HERRING

Real Baltic herring are only found in the mid-Baltic. Baltic herring are actually a smaller version of regular herring and the line between where herring and Baltic herring is caught is said to extend out from Kalmar.

Because of this you can't find Baltic herring outside the borders of Scandinavia. However, to my great joy, you can find fish that are close relatives. Smelt are closest in both taste and size. Sardines can be used in an emergency, even if the taste isn't the same. So I have my craving satisfied when the desire for Baltic herring hits. It has a delicate flavor that all but the fussiest palates can appreciate. Since I come from Västergötland, I always want lingonberries, even with Baltic herring—we eat lingonberries with everything there!

Baltic Herring with Mashed Potatoes

2 lbs. smelt (sardines can be used in a pinch)
1 cup dried breadcrumbs or rye flour, or a combination of both
1 tsp. salt
parsley

plenty of butter for sautéing

- Begin by boiling the potatoes for mashed potatoes.
- Remove the heads and the tails from the fish. Clean and rinse the fish and remove the backbone. Cut off the back fin.
- Combine the dried breadcrumbs and, if using, the rye flour on a plate and stir in the salt.
- Dredge the pieces of fish in the dried breadcrumbs.
- Sauté them immediately in plenty of butter.
- Sprinkle chopped parsley over fish. Serve with mashed potatoes. Lingonberry preserves also make a tasty accompaniment.

Pickled Baltic Herring

6 fried smelt filets
2 cups water
10 tbsp. 5% distilled vinegar
6 tbsp. sugar

2 tsp. salt
2 tsp. allspice corns
2 red onions
4 bay leaves

- Boil the water, sugar, salt and distilled vinegar until the sugar dissolves. Leave to cool.
- Slice the onions.
- Place some of the fried Baltic herring (or smelt) filets in a glass jar. Alternate layers of herring with layers of onion.
- Crush the allspice corns in a mortar and pestle. Add to brine.
- Pour the brine over the herring and onions.
- Add the bay leaves.
- Cover and let the herring stand steep in the refrigerator for half a day.

Ladies' Week

Sweden's Ladies' Week occurs during the week of the 19th to the 24th of July. This is when the name days for Sara, Margareta, Johanna, Magdalena, Emma and Kristina fall. In some places they add Jacob or Fredrik to the list to make it a whole week. Name days are a sort of mini-birthday, usually celebrated with a cake. Each day of the year has been given a name, and a few years ago the number of names was increased by adding similar names to each day. It typically rains during Ladies' Week. Some people claim it is the week with the highest precipitation all year. I don't know if I agree, though. I remember mostly that the days were mostly sunny when we sat in the garden eating cake to celebrate my sister Johanna's name day.

PRINCESS TORTE

If you like marzipan with whipped cream, then princess torte is a dream. It is a Swedish favorite, sold at cafés and bakeries throughout the country. Baking your own princess torte takes a little time and has its challenges. But I promise everyone, yes, everyone will be deeply impressed by its grand appearance and its delicious taste. Both Swedish princesses Victoria and Madeleine have certainly tasted a few princess tortes on their birthdays, which both fall in the summer.

Cake base

4 eggs
1 2/3 cups sugar
3/4 cup hot water
2 tsp. baking powder
1 2/3 cup all-purpose flour

Oven temperature: 350° F
Raspberry or raspberry jam

- Beat the eggs and sugar until fluffy.
- Heat the water and stir into the egg mixture.
- Mix the flour and baking powder in a separate bowl.
- Fold into wet mixture.
- Pour the batter into a round 9 x 3 1/2-inch greased cake pan.
- Bake for 30-40 minutes.
- Let the cake cool and slice it into three layers. Spread raspberry jam or place fresh raspberries with a little sugar sprinkled on them on the bottom layer.
- The second layer gets covered with half the cream filling (see below).
- Place the third layer on top and then spread the rest of the cream filling on top and down over the sides so the whole cake is covered.
- Now there is only the marzipan left.

Cream filling

1 1/4 cup whole milk
2 egg yolks
1 tbsp. sugar
1 tbsp. cornstarch
1 1/2 tsp. vanilla extract
1 envelope gelatin
1 1/4 cups heavy cream

- Pour the milk into a heavy-bottomed pan. Add the egg yolks, sugar and cornstarch. Warm the mixture over medium low heat, stirring constantly until it thickens. Add the vanilla extract. Dissolve the gelatin in a little water and add it to the mixture.
- Set aside, stirring it from time to time as it cools.
- Whip the heavy cream. Carefully blend into cooled filling mixture.

Marzipan

14 oz marzipan
green, yellow and red food coloring
powdered sugar

- Set aside a little marzipan for making a rose.
- Place the rest of the marzipan in a medium-sized plastic food storage bag. Make a little indentation in the marzipan and add 3 drops of green food coloring and one drop of the yellow. Knead the marzipan in the plastic bag until it is evenly colored.
- Lay out a large piece of plastic wrap and put the marzipan on it. Cut open a plastic food storage bag so that it is large enough to cover the marzipan, place over marzipan and roll out. This is a great way to avoid having the marzipan stick to the rolling pin.
- Roll out marzipan into a thin, circular sheet large enough to drape over and cover the whole cake. Tip: trace the bottom of the cake pan onto paper, then measure the height of the cake and add it to the pan diameter to calculate the total diameter for your marzipan sheet. This way the marzipan is large enough to cover the whole cake.
- Peel the plastic bag off the top of the marzipan sheet, then turn the mar-

zipan so that the side that was on the plastic wrap facing upward. Remove the plastic carefully. Pinch in the edges and trim away the excess marzipan.
- Take the reserved piece of marzipan and add a drop of red food coloring. Knead it until it turns pink and cut out a rose or another decoration of your choice and place on top of the cake.
- Sprinkle the cake with powdered sugar.

PINOCCHIO CAKE

This was one of my favorite cakes as a child. I remember my mother would get it from a little bakery in Ulricehamn called Skånebageriet where she was acquainted with one of the shop assistants.

5 tbsp. butter
5 egg yolks
3/4 cup powdered sugar
2/3 cup all-purpose flour
1 1/2 tsp. baking powder
4 tbsp. whole milk

5 egg whites
3/4 cup sugar
slivered almonds

1 1/4 cups heavy cream

Oven temperature: 350° F

- Line a 12 x 16-inch cake pan with baking parchment and butter well.
- Mix the butter and powdered sugar in a bowl until fluffy. Add one egg yolk at a time, blending after each. Save the egg whites for the meringue.
- Mix the flour and baking powder in a bowl then fold into wet mixture.
- Add the milk and stir well.
- Transfer the batter to the pan.
- Beat the egg whites in another bowl until stiff, fold in the sugar and beat again.
- Spread the egg whites over the batter, creating a somewhat tufted surface.
- Sprinkle the slivered almonds on top.
- Bake on the middle or lower shelf of the oven until the meringue is lightly browned and the cake is dry, approximately 20 minutes.
- Take the cake out, let cool before removing the baking paper. Cut horizontally to divide the cake into two pieces.
- Whip the cream and spread it over the bottom piece. Place the other layer on top.

TOSCA CAKE

Cake base

plain breadcrumbs
2 eggs
2/3 cup sugar
3/4 cup all-purpose flour
1/4 cup whole milk or heavy cream
1 tsp. baking powder
4 oz butter or margarine

Glaze

1/2 cup sugar
2 tbsp. all-purpose flour
2 tbsp. whole milk
4 oz butter or margarine
2/3 cup sliced almonds

Oven temperature: 350° F

- Butter and coat a springform cake pan with plain breadcrumbs to keep the cake from sticking.
- Melt the butter for the cake.
- Beat the eggs and sugar together until fluffy.
- In a separate bowl combine flour and baking powder.
- Fold the butter, dry mixture and milk into the wet mixture.
- Transfer batter to pan.
- Bake the cake on the lower shelf of the oven 20-25 minutes.
- While the cake is baking, make the glaze.
- Combine the butter, sugar, flour and milk in a heavy-bottomed saucepan.
- Warm the mixture carefully, stirring the whole time until it thickens.
- When the glaze has thickened, stir in the almonds.
- Take the cake out of the oven and spread the glaze on top.
- Return the cake to the middle shelf of the oven and continue baking until golden brown.
- Serve the cake with whipped cream.

ALMOND CAKE

Cake base

  7 oz almond paste
  2 egg whites
  or
  1/3 cup blanched almonds
  1/3 cup sugar
  2 egg whites

Butter cream

  4 egg yolks
  1/2 cup sugar
  1/2 cup heavy cream
  4 oz butter
  slivered almonds for garnish

Oven temperature: 350° F

- Blanche and peel the almonds, if necessary, and grind them.
- Beat the egg whites until stiff. Save the egg yolks for the butter cream.
- Combine the sugar with the ground almonds into a dish. If using almond paste, grate it on a grater or use a food processor. Carefully fold almond/sugar mixture or almond paste into the egg whites.
- Spread the batter on the baking paper, forming a circle, 10 inches in diameter.
- Bake the cake on the middle shelf of the oven for approximately 15 minutes.
- Loosen the cake from the baking paper.

Butter cream

- Combine the egg yolks, cream, sugar and butter in a saucepan. Let the mixture simmer, stirring constantly until it thickens.
- Let the mixture cool.
- Spread the butter cream on the almond cake.
- Decorate with slivered almonds.

STRAWBERRY CAKE

This is the quintessential summer dessert, especially on Midsummer Eve.

Cake base

4 eggs
1 2/3 cup sugar
3/4 cup hot water
2 tsp. vanilla extract
2 tsp. baking powder
1 2/3 cups all-purpose flour

Oven temperature: 350° F

1 1/4 cups heavy cream
3 lb strawberries
sugar

- Beat the eggs and sugar until fluffy.
- Heat the water and add it to the eggs and sugar together with the vanilla extract.
- Combine the flour and baking powder in a separate bowl.
- Fold into wet ingredients.
- Pour the batter into a greased round 9 x 3 1/2-inch cake pan.
- Bake for 30-40 minutes.
- Turn the cake out onto a cutting board and let it cool before slicing horizontally into three layers.
- Slice 2 lbs. of the strawberries, sprinkle with sugar and arrange them between the cake layers. Place the cake in the refrigerator (for a few hours, if possible), so that it has a chance to absorb some of the strawberry juice. This makes it extra moist.
- Whip the cream. Cover the whole cake with whipped cream.
- Garnish with the rest of the strawberries.

AGNETA'S U.S.A. CAKE

Agneta is a good friend who has a wonderful view over Central Park in New York City. Her home is always open to guests and when she throws parties she often makes this fantastic cake. It's a delectable treat, filled with mounds of berries – you can't forget your first bite. Actually, Agneta's mother originated this recipe. Ever since September 11 the cake has become even more American, since it is often decorated like an American flag.

6 eggs
2 1/2 cups sugar
2 1/2 cups all-purpose flour
2/3 cup hot water
6 tsp. baking powder
dried breadcrumbs and butter for greasing the pan
fresh berries to mix into the batter (to taste, optional)
fresh berries to place between layers: Agneta suggests 1-1 1/2 pints of frozen or fresh berries between the cake layers, preferably a mix of crushed strawberries, blueberries and raspberries.

raspberries and blueberries for decoration

1 pint heavy cream

Oven temperature: 350° - 400° F

- Beat the eggs and sugar in a mixing bowl until fluffy.
- Add hot water.
- Blend the baking powder and flour in a separate bowl, then fold into wet mixture.
- Add some berries to the batter, if desired.
- Butter two baking pans, approximately 10 x 12-inch, and coat them with breadcrumbs.
- Divide the batter evenly between the two pans.
- Bake until golden brown, 30-40 minutes.
- Cover one cake with whipped cream, then lots of berries.
- Place the other cake on top and decorate with whipped cream and berries – use red and blue berries to make an American flag pattern if desired.

144

"SAFT" – FRUIT SYRUP DRINK

"Saft" is a very traditional drink loved by Swedes of all ages. You can adjust the strength to taste by adjusting the amount of water used. If I have the choice between a glass of soda and a glass of "saft", the choice is easy. Not least because I know it is made from fresh berries.

2 lb cleaned berries
Strawberries, raspberries, rhubarb, black and red currants or cherries are great
1 2/3 cups water

1 quart extracted juice
2 cups sugar

- Carefully rinse and slice berries.
- Add berries to boiling water and boil vigorously until they are soft, about 10 minutes. Stir to prevent berries from sticking. Add extra water if needed.
- Strain the berries through a cheese cloth into a large bowl. If you don't have a cheese cloth, line a large strainer with a piece of sheeting. Hold the cloth in place with clips.
- After the berries have cooled substantially you can squeeze the cheese cloth a bit to get all the juice completely out.
- Measure the amount of strained juice to balance the amount of juice and sugar (some berries contain more liquid than others).
- Bring juice to a boil in a saucepan, then add the sugar.
- Skim the film that forms on top; keep a bowl of water next to the stove to rinse the film off your skimming spoon.
- Boil until sugar is dissolved. Let the fruit syrup cool a little before transferring to a sterilized bottle, preferably one with a screw top (such as for canning).
- Keep the fruit syrup in the refrigerator.
- To serve, mix approximately one part fruit syrup to nine parts water.

VEGETABLE SOUP

My mother used to make large batches of this soup so there would be vegetable soup all week long afterward.

2-3 carrots
1 leek
1 head cauliflower
1 parsnip
6 cups vegetable bouillon
3/4 cup frozen peas
3 tbsp. butter
parsley
salt and pepper according to taste

- Finely cut the carrots, parsnip and leek in slices. Break the cauliflower into smaller pieces.

- Melt the butter in a large pot. Do not let it brown.
- Add all vegetables, except for the leek, parsley and peas, to pan.
- Salt and pepper according to taste.
- Add bouillon.
- Boil 10-15 minutes until the vegetables are cooked through but not falling apart.
- Add the leek, parsley and peas just before serving.

149

POTATO LEEK SOUP

This is perfect in both summer and winter, served cold or warm. It is extra tasty if you add a dollop of sour cream.

4-5 medium potatoes
2 large leeks
6 cups beef or chicken bouillon
1 tbsp. freshly squeezed lemon juice
1 clove pressed garlic
salt and white pepper according to taste

- Peel and cut the potatoes into small cubes.
- Rinse the leeks carefully. Cut them into small pieces.
- Bring to a boil and then simmer the potatoes and leeks in the bouillon over low heat for 15-20 minutes.
- Mash the potatoes and leeks with an electric mixer or food processor.
- Add the lemon juice and pressed garlic.
- Season with pepper and salt.
- The soup may be served either warm or cold, preferably with a dollop of sour cream.

SALMON PUDDING

Almost any salmon dish is guaranteed to be a success. This dish belongs at the top of the list. If you decide to mildly cure salmon, it may be worth making a little extra so that there is also enough for salmon pudding. If you can't make or get hold of mildly cured salmon and want to make salmon pudding right away, use gravlax or smoked salmon.

10 oz mildly cured lax (see recipe p. 94), smoked salmon or gravlax may be substituted
8 potatoes
1 large yellow onion
2-3 tbsp. of finely chopped dill
1 2/3 cups whole milk
3 eggs
a pinch of pepper
butter for greasing casserole dish
2-4 oz melted butter for serving

Oven temperature: 425° F

- Butter an 8 x 12-inch ovenproof casserole dish.
- Peel and slice the potatoes.
- Chop the onion and sauté it lightly in a little butter.
- Cut the salmon into thin slices.
- Layer the potatoes, salmon, onion and dill in the ovenproof dish. The top and bottom layers should be potatoes.
- Beat together the milk and the egg. Season with a little white pepper. Pour this mixture into the baking dish.
- Bake on the lower rack of the oven until the egg mixture has set and the potatoes are soft, approximately 40 minutes. Cover the dish with aluminum foil for the first 20 minutes of cooking time.
- Serve with melted butter.

Crayfish

We Swedes love to guzzle down crayfish by the light of the shining crayfish moon lanterns. August 8 was, for a long time, the official beginning of crayfish season. Crayfish fishing wasn't allowed year-round so the crayfish could reach their full size in peace and quiet.

When I was little, August 8 was a magical date. It meant that we would go down to the little brook near where my grandparents lived. The brook was almost invisible because there were so many reeds growing around it, and one could hardly imagine that there would be crayfish in it. Papa would tell us how, when he was little, the brook was teeming with crayfish and they would pull up traps that were entirely black with the small creatures. I don't know if our traps were quite so black with them, but we would catch scores of them, in any case (the number of crayfish caught is usually counted in scores). We used both traps and nets. If you used nets, you had to check them a lot because the rascals could escape from them. Roach was the fish we used as bait, and we would pick it up on our way there at one of my father's cousin's.

The little road down to the brook was bumpy, to say the least, and you had to open several gates before you finally came down to an open space. Collapsible coffee tables were set up, and small campstools of faded blue and red cloth. I remember them so well. When the traps and nets had been laid out we would all sit down and take a break for a moment to drink coffee and saft, a fruit syrup drink, and eat sandwiches. We always had egg and anchovy sandwiches on sweet limpa bread, I remember. They were good, and I still love to make them, though here in the U.S. I use Matjes herring instead, since anchovies in oil don't taste the same. After the break we would pull out the plastic buckets and check the traps. We had a special stick to pull them up through the reeds. It was always exciting to see if we had caught anything. It was a little scary to try and pull the crayfish out; they had strong claws, I had felt them once when they pinched me. When the light began to go, we would use a flashlight, and that was probably what we liked most as children. Finally, we would give up and I remember how I would examine the crayfish carefully the whole way home.

The crayfish were cooked up in a big pot the next day. I wasn't as fond of that. I felt so sorry for the crayfish, who had by this time become my friends. We had to throw them in one at a time to keep the water hot enough to kill them right away. The method for cooking crayfish in Sweden is quite different from the American way. The most important ingredient is crown dill, a product that I've noticed is rarely found in the U.S., although the florist's shop might have it. I have also cooked my crayfish with regular dill and a little sugar and salt and they turned out well too.

Fishing for crayfish isn't the only way we got crayfish in our family. My grandfather, who ran his own company, didn't have time to go through the trouble of fishing for a few crayfish. He simply bought them. I remember going along with him in a car to pick them up. I remember especially well the time when the crayfish escaped and ended up all over the car; I had a tough job gathering them up without getting pinched. That was some trip!

Today things don't look so good for crayfish. In Sweden, crayfish blight killed almost all the native crayfish. Now we've managed to repair nearly all that damage by stocking the waters with new crayfish. I wrote countless articles about this when I began my career as a journalist for a local paper, the *Arboga Tidning*. One of the hottest debates was whether they should have crayfish or eels in Hjälmaren,

Sweden's fourth largest lake. They couldn't have both because, as it happened, they would eat each other up.

When crayfish season arrives, you can buy Turkish, Chinese, and American crayfish for a reasonable sum in the grocery store, cooked the true Swedish way. And I must say, they are actually really good. On Gotland, mainly to pamper ourselves, we buy a score of genuine Swedish native crayfish, which are not quite as cheap. Gotland is, in fact, one of the few places where there are still native crayfish to be caught. Of course, it's really fun to eat these

were a very popular food, something which the bard Bellman sang of. At that time, people didn't eat the crayfish whole as we do today. Instead they ate them in the form of crayfish cakes, crayfish sausage, and crayfish tails prepared in all sorts of ways. When they did eat crayfish whole, they ate them warm.

The custom of letting crayfish cool in their own stock and cooking them with crown dill is something that first became popular at the end of the 1800s. It was during this time that the popularity of crayfish rose drastically and laws were created to protect the crayfish population from overfishing. Today, these restrictions are gone, but still most people choose to wait until the beginning of August to eat crayfish. The phenomenon of the crayfish party started in the 1930s, when it became a sort of farewell-to-summer party, celebrating the summer weather outdoors, preferably with funny hats.

The third Thursday in August is the beginning of fermented Baltic herring season. Fermented Baltic herring is a delicacy according to some, or completely the opposite according to others. Baltic herring makes its home along the coast of Norrland and the fermented version became known as early as the 1500s as a poor man's dish. Three hundred years later, the fermented, yeasty fish managed to find its way into the finer salons and was transformed into a party food. Personally, I feel very divided regarding this fish; the stench released upon opening the can really makes you wonder

while wearing crayfish hats beneath paper crayfish moon lanterns with one or two glasses of schnapps. This is all part of the celebration, just like toasted bread and, of course, the slurping, for God knows how much we have to slurp to get all the good crayfish stock.

Eating crayfish in Sweden has been popular for centuries. In medieval times monks used to consume enormous amounts of crayfish during Lent. Crayfish can even claim ancient royal ancestry. King Erik XIV cultivated crayfish, among other things, in the moats around Kalmar Castle. During the 1700s, crayfish

about the wisdom of eating the contents. Baltic herring are caught in the spring when they're spawning. After being gutted, they are placed in heavily salted water for forty-eight hours, then moved to milder brine, where they remain for six to eight weeks to ferment. After fermentation the Baltic herring are packed in tins.

With the stench in mind, most fermented herring parties are held outdoors. To be really honest, the fish doesn't smell that bad if you just make sure to open the tins well ahead of time. Absolutely necessary accompaniments are "Mandelpotatis", a sort of potato, thin bread (soft or hard), as well as red onions, and, of cour-se, you have to have the obligatory schnapps and beer.

In southern Sweden the occasion that corresponds to a fermented Baltic herring party is an eel feast. At these, plenty of eels are prepared in many ways. Between the bites of fat eel a glass or two of schnapps is slipped down. At the eel feasts also feature an eel king and an eel queen, titles awarded to the man and woman who were the quickest to pull an eel out of a dark barrel in a dark room. One can read about this and many other things in Skåne author Frithiof Nilsson Piraten's books.

CRAYFISH

2 lb live crayfish
8 cups water
4 tbsp. salt
1 tbsp. sugar
lots of dill, including the stalks, preferably
with the heads

- Boil the water with the sugar, salt and dill.
- Make sure the water has come to a full boil
  before you add the crayfish, one by one.
  This is to ensure that the cooking temperature stays as high as possible so the crayfish
  die instantly.
- Let the crayfish boil 6-10 minutes. Then let
  them cool in their own stock, after the last
  one has been added.
- You can even boil up previously cooked
  crayfish in the same way to revive their taste.

Autumn's Darkness Falls

The days grow shorter, the evenings darker, and the leaves begin to turn. We have to admit that the glorious summer is reaching its end and fall is beginning to enter the scene. Many Swedes have on their agenda one last desperate attempt to hold onto summer by making jams and fruit syrups with the garden's bounty. People do the same with everything they can find growing in the woods or in the ground. That's when I think of lingonberries, blueberries, cloudberries, and mushrooms.

Pulling on rubber boots and marching out to the woods in search of mushrooms is an experience that appeals to many, especially if you find chanterelles. It's important to know which mushrooms are edible and which are poisonous. In our family, we usually satisfy ourselves with chanterelles because they don't look like any other mushroom. Chanterelles sautéed in butter and served on toast are utterly delicious. Oh, how I miss them sometimes! If you found a lot of them, you might take the trouble to dry or parboil them in order to bring them out weeks or months later and remember summer while the autumn storms advance.

We also used to freeze large quantities of lingonberries so we could make them into preserves during the rest of the year. Lingonberries are something that we Swedes love. The red berries strongly resemble cranberries in both appearance and taste but they are a little bit smaller in size. My grandmother used to make "saft" (fruit syrup) and jelly from the currants in the garden; she was a master with jelly. We also made "saft" from strawberries before they disappeared. "Saft" is a very popular drink in Sweden, and for many a substitute to soda. When I was little, Coca-cola was a rare thing that you ordered if you went out to a café. I must say that drinking soda is much more common among contemporary Swedish children and youth; however, I still persist in serving homemade "saft" and lingonberry juice at home.

In olden times, people celebrated Michaelmas on September 29th, St. Michael's Day, a day that used to be called the autumnal equinox. It was the day people were permitted to begin lighting candles indoors again. Hopefully, all the crops would be in a shed or barn,

166

and the livestock could also move indoors again. Herders would come walking back from the summer pastures, blowing crumhorns and other horns to herd their cows home. St. Michael was the archangel renowned as the dragon slayer. He also took care of souls when they left their earthly existence and decided if they had earned a place in paradise.

Pantries were well filled when Michaelmas came around, which resulted in a true harvest feast. People often allowed themselves something extra for the festivities. It was common to slaughter sheep for Michaelmas, and in Västmanland people would prepare a large pot of lamb stew and place it on the table for guests to enjoy with freshly brewed beer and aquavit. People danced and partied wildly, often for three days. Michaelmas was the holiday when the old was finished to make way for the new. Old grudges were left behind to make room for fresh, positive energy. The church held special services during which people gave thanks for the harvest they had received, and the banns were read for those who had decided to embark on marriage.

For farmhands and maids, Michaelmas was really their only week off. They could visit their families, and they received a gift of food from the master and mistress of the house that would tide them over for several days. If servants had decided to change masters, Michaelmas was the day this change would occur. They were required to inform their masters at least three months in advance. Since the harvest wasn't always completely in by Michaelmas, this date for changing jobs wasn't especially popular, and in the mid 1800s the date was changed to October 24th. The big "holiday killer" King Gustav III, had already changed Michaelmas to a holiday held on the first Sunday following September 29th. October, is also moose-hunting season, an activity that many seem to enjoy. Moose towers are built along the woods' edge and hunters sit in them and watch for their quarry. Each hunting club is given a quota depending on how large the moose population is. In Västergötland, where I grew up, moose are numerous and you have to be unbelievably attentive driving at dusk and dawn when they tend to appear.

The moose is called the king of the forest, which you understand when you get close to one. What big, strapping fellows they are! Colliding with a moose is comparable to driving into a stone wall. Their long legs mean that the whole moose usually hits the windshield, which can have fatal consequences. Every year many motorists die, although wildlife fences are being erected and hunting promoted to keep the moose population in check. The meat from the slain moose is divided up among the hunting club members and the owner of the land gets his share as well. A moose dinner is a real delicacy, although until recently it was necessary to have good connections with hunters or landowners in order to enjoy it; it has actually started to appear in grocery stores but it is rather expensive.

APPLE PIE

With the fall comes the harvest of all the berries and fruits, among them apples.
My own favorite of the endless varieties of apple pie and apple cake is without a
doubt apple crumb pie. Not only that, it is incredibly simple to make, and truly
delicious made with any kind of fruit.

5 apples
3 tbsp. sugar
1 tsp. cinnamon

Crumb dough

1 cup all–purpose flour
1 tbsp. sugar
4 oz butter or margarine

Oven temperature: 425° F

- Begin by making the crumb dough.
  Combine the flour and sugar, then
  add the butter or margarine. Use a
  fork or work it in with your fingers
  until the dough has a crumb-like
  texture. It is not supposed to stick
  together.
- Peel and core the apples, then slice
  them.
- Butter an ovenproof pie pan.
- Place the apple slices in the dish,
  sprinkling sugar and cinnamon
  between the apple layers.

- Sprinkle the crumb dough over the
  top of the apples and bake the pie in
  the oven until it has turned golden
  brown, about 20 minutes.
- Serve the apple pie warm with vanilla sauce or whipped cream.

Vanilla Sauce

2 egg yolks
1 2/3 cups whole milk
3 tsp. cornstarch
1 tbsp. vanilla extract
2 tbsp. sugar

- Combine all the ingredients except
  the vanilla in a saucepan (avoid aluminum saucepans if possible).
- Let the mixture simmer over low
  heat, stirring constantly with a
  whisk.
- When the mixture is thick enough,
  place the saucepan in cold water in
  the sink, keep stirring until it cools.
- Add the vanilla extract.

CINNAMON BUNS

You can't find anything more Swedish than cinnamon buns. They were invented in the 1920s, right after the end of the First World War when there was plenty of both sugar and butter. The bakers wanted to come up with something special and decided that buns were extra good filled with a mixture of cinnamon, sugar and butter, which was then rolled up into a bun. As an added luxury a little pearl sugar was sprinkled on top.

Makes about 40 buns

    2 cups whole milk
    4 oz butter or margarine
    2 packages active dry yeast
    1/2 tsp. salt
    2/3 cup sugar
    5-6 cups all-purpose flour

Filling

    4 oz butter or margarine at room temperature
    1/2 cup sugar
    2 tbsp. ground cinnamon

    1 beaten egg and pearl sugar for garnish

Oven temperature: 425-450° F

- Melt the butter or margarine in a large pan and add the milk. Let the mixture reach a lukewarm temperature. Remove from the heat.
- Stir the yeast into the liquid and make sure it is well blended.
- Add the salt and sugar.
- Mix in half the flour and stir. Then add the rest of the flour, stirring until the dough is no longer sticky.
- Knead the dough for a couple of minutes, then put it back in the pan and let it rise under a cloth for 30-45 minutes.
- While the dough is rising, mix all the ingredients for the filling in a bowl. Stir until the butter is completely soft and blended with the cinnamon and sugar.
- Divide the dough in two. Begin by rolling out one part into a 15" by 15" square.
- Spread half of the filling over the rolled-out dough. When the dough is completely covered, roll it up.
- Slice into approximately 15-20 pieces. Repeat with the other half of the dough.
- Place them in paper muffin cups with the swirl pattern facing up.
- Let them rise about 30 minutes under a cloth.
- Brush the buns with a beaten egg. Decorate with pearl sugar if you can get it. It is available in Scandinavian shops and at Ikea.
- If pearl sugar is not available, you can brush the baked buns just before serving with a little melted butter and dip them in granulated sugar.
- Bake the buns in the oven about 5 minutes until they turn a golden brown.

POTATO DUMPLINGS

Potato dumplings from Öland and Småland and those from Norrland are all close-ly related. Which one is best probably depends on whom you ask. They differ from each other somewhat; the dumplings from Öland are made with raw potatoes, while the ones from Småland are made with boiled. "Pitepalt", the most well known of all the dumplings from Norrland, are prepared like the potato dump-lings from Öland, with raw potatoes, and barley is used in addition to wheat flour.

8-10 potatoes
1 egg
1 cup all-purpose flour
1 tsp. salt

Filling

8 oz lightly cured pork or, alternati-vely, bacon
1 large yellow onion
1 1/2 tsp. crushed allspice
a pinch of salt (optional)
lots of water for cooking (4-5 pints)
1/2 tsp. salt per pint of water

- Peel and boil the potatoes.
- While the potatoes are cooking pre-pare the filling.
- Finely dice pork or bacon.
- Peel and mince the onion.
- Crush the allspice with a mortar and pestle.
- Fry the pork or bacon. Add the oni-on when almost done. Sprinkle with the allspice.

- Set this mixture aside.
- When the potatoes are cooked, pour off the water and let them cool a little.
- Press the potatoes through a ricer.
- Add the flour and egg to the riced potatoes. Season with salt.
- Mix the dough with your hands until smooth.
- Shape the dough into a long roll and divide it into 12 parts.
- Mold these into balls and make a small indentation in the middle of each one.
- Fill the indentation with a little of the meat mixture and close it up.
- Boil water in a large pot.
- Add in a few potato dumplings at time. When they float to the surface they are done (approx. 5 minutes).
- Serve with melted butter and ling-onberry preserves.

SMÅLAND CHEESECAKE

In Småland cheesecake has long been the dessert of choice, the pride of every farmer's wife, with origins all the way back to the 1600s. Today there are perhaps not as many who make their own cheesecake since it is available to buy in the frozen food aisle. All you have to do is whip the cream and set out raspberry or strawberry preserves. Just like potato dumplings, Norrland and Hälsingland have their own versions.

4-5 portions

2 eggs
4 tbsp. all-purpose flour
1/4 cup heavy cream
1 cup whole milk
1/4 cup blanched, chopped almonds
1 lb. cottage cheese
3 tbsp. sugar
butter to butter the dish with

Oven temperature: 350° F

- Blanche and chop the almonds.
- Beat the eggs, flour, cream and milk into a batter.
- Stir in the almonds and cottage cheese.
- Pour the batter into an ovenproof dish. Bake on the middle rack of the oven about 50 minutes until the cheesecake has turned golden brown.

SAILOR'S BEEF

Here we have meat, sauce and potatoes in the same pot. One can understand how this meal would be ideal to eat at sea.

1 lb boneless round steak in thin slices
2-3 tbsp. butter or margarine
1-2 tsp. salt
a pinch of white pepper
1 tsp. allspice, crushed with a mortar and pestle
3-4 yellow onions, sliced in rings
8-10 potatoes, peeled and sliced
12 oz port or dark beer
1 cup water

- Peel and slice the potatoes.
- Brown the steak lightly on both sides in the butter.
- Add water and let it cook down so that pan juices form.
- Lightly brown the onions.
- Layer the potatoes, onion and beef in a large pot. Make sure the bottom and top layers are potatoes. Season each layer. Pour the pan juices over the top as well as a bottle of port.
- Let simmer over low heat with the lid on for 30-40 minutes.

SALT PORK WITH ONION SAUCE

Onion Sauce

    2 medium-sized yellow onions
    2 tbsp. butter or margarine
    2 tbsp. all-purpose flour
    1 2/3 cups whole milk
    salt and white pepper

- Peel and finely chop the onion.
- Melt the butter in a saucepan and sauté the onions until soft.
- Mix the flour in some milk and pour it over the onions, stirring as you do.
- Continue to stir and add more milk until the sauce reaches the desired consistency.
- Season with salt and white pepper.
- Serve with boiled potatoes and fried salt pork or bacon.

BROWN BEANS WITH SALT PORK

Brown beans have been grown since the 1800s on Öland, Sweden's second largest island. It was probably some immigrant from Öland to America who got the idea of bringing back some brown beans to Sweden. Öland is singularly suited for cultivating these brown beans. The soil is rich in lime and the hours of sunshine more numerous there than in many other places in summertime Sweden.

1 can pinto beans
1 1/2 tbsp. 5% distilled vinegar
2 tbsp. sugar or corn syrup
1/2 tsp. salt
1 tbsp. cornstarch
water

- Boil the beans in a little water.
- Mix the cornstarch in a little water and add to the beans.
- If it gets too thick add more water.
- Season with salt, sugar and distilled vinegar.
- Serve the beans with boiled potatoes and fried salt pork or bacon.

CABBAGE SOUP WITH QUENELLES

Cabbage soup was very common once upon a time when everyone grew his or her own cabbage and kept it in an earth cellar so it could be eaten year round. Cabbage soup made a solid meal for little money. Forcemeat balls, or quenelles, added a little extra touch to the soup.

Cabbage Soup

1/2 medium heads of white cabbage
4 cups beef bouillon (4 cups water +
2 bouillon cubes)
4 allspice corns
a pinch of white pepper
1 bay leaf
salt

- Rinse the cabbage and shred it.
- Bring the bouillon and spices to a boil.
- Add the cabbage and boil until the cabbage is soft, about 20 minutes.
- Add salt to taste.

Quenelles

1/2 lb ground veal or ground beef
1 tbsp. dried breadcrumbs
1/3 cup whole milk
1/2 tsp. salt
1/8 tsp. white pepper
1 egg
2 cups chicken bouillon (2 cups water plus 1 chicken bouillon cube)

- Mix the dried breadcrumbs with the milk and let them expand.
- Combine the ground meat, spices and egg. Work the mixture until it is smooth, with a slightly mushy consistency.
- Form small balls. Tip: Keep a bowl of water close by to dip your hands into because the consistency is mushy.
- Boil quenelles in chicken bouillon for about 5 minutes. Then put them

STUFFED CABBAGE ROLLS

Stuffed cabbage rolls seem completely Swedish to me, though actually they have Turkish origins. Opinion is devided as to whether these tasty treats caught on when King Karl the XII and his soldiers were inspired by the stuffed grape leaves eaten during the fray at Bender in 1713, or during the Turks' stay in Stockholm afterwards to negotiate war debts. But since grape leaves are rare in Swedish latitudes, cabbage leaves had to be substituted. The original lemon sauce was also switched to domestic lingonberry. Thus, a Swedish classic was born, with a little Turkish influence.

Makes approximately 30

> 1 medium head white cabbage (2-3 lb)
> 1 lb ground beef
> 2/3 cup Japanese rice
> 1/4 tsp. white pepper
> 1 tsp. ground allspice
> 1-1 1/2 tsp. salt
> 2/3 cup whole milk
> optional: 1 tbsp. corn syrup to drizzle over the cabbage rolls during cooking
> butter to butter the baking dish with

Oven temperature: 425° F

- Cook the rice according to the directions on the package and let cool.
- Combine the ground meat, rice, spices and milk in a mixing bowl and stir well.
- Boil the water in a large pan.
- Make a few incisions around the stalk of the cabbage head so the leaves loosen up more easily when it boils.
- Place the cabbage head in the boiling water and let it boil about 5-10 minutes.
- Remove the cabbage from the boiling water and let it cool.
- Reserve about two cups of the cooking water.
- Carefully loosen the cabbage leaves so they remain whole.
- Place a mound, about 2-3 tbsp., of the ground meat mixture on each cabbage leaf, pinch up the sides and fold into a roll.
- Tie a piece of cotton thread around each bundle so it stays together.
- Butter a roasting pan or, alternatively, a large aluminum pan and place the stuffed cabbage rolls in it.
- Pour a little cabbage stock over the cabbage rolls so they don't stick, then drizzle about 1 tbsp. corn syrup over them.

- Let the cabbage rolls cook until they have turned golden brown, about an hour, turning occasionally.
- Serve with boiled potatoes, the following sauce and lingonberry preserves.

Sauce

2 1/2 cups cabbage stock: the pan juices from the baked cabbage rolls combined with the reserved cooking water from boiling the cabbage.
1 beef bouillon cube

2 tbsp. all-purpose flour
2 tsp. brown sugar
1 tbsp. heavy cream
a little soy sauce (optional)
salt and white pepper

- Bring the cabbage stock to a boil.
- Whisk in the flour. Add the heavy cream.
- Let the mixture thicken slightly stirring continuously.
- Season with brown sugar, soy sauce, salt and white pepper.

SALMON TROUT WITH FISH ROE SAUCE

Salmon trout is a fish most often associated with Norrland, the northern part of Sweden. That is why it's not so strange that it was my friend Lotta from Norrland who introduced me to this dish.

1 salmon trout per person
salt and pepper

Oven temperature: 350° F

- Scale, clean and rinse the fish. If you leave the heads on, remove the gills.
- Salt and pepper the fish. Wrap each fish in aluminum foil.
- Place them directly on the oven rack.
- Bake the fish about 20-30 minutes, cooking time depending on the size of the fish.
- Serve with fish roe sauce and riced potatoes.

Fish roe sauce

3/4 cup sour cream
1/2 red onion
1 tbsp. red caviar

- Finely chop the red onion.
- Stir the onion into the sour cream.
- Carefully fold the caviar into the sauce.

BEEF À LA LINDSTRÖM

There is disagreement as to which Lindström can take the credit for this beloved beef dish. No fewer than four Lindströms are competing for the honor of having invented the national dish. One thing that is clear is that it draws inspiration from Russian food with its red beets and capers. So Lieutenant Lindström is probably a good candidate. He grew up in Russia and during his time in Kalmar he took his meals at the Hotel Witt where he inspired the chef to prepare beef in the Russian manner, incorporating onions, capers and beets.

1 lb ground beef
1 egg
1/4 cup heavy cream
1 finely chopped boiled potatoes (cold)
1/3 cup finely chopped pickled beets (see recipe, p. 30)
2 tbsp. minced yellow onion
2 tbsp. minced capers
1 tsp. salt
white pepper

butter or margarine for frying

Sauce:
1 cup water
1 cube beef bouillon
2 tbsp. liquid from the pickled beets
few drops of liquid from the capers

- Begin by boiling and chopping the potato. (If you like, you can also boil potatoes to serve with the beef.)
- Thoroughly combine all the ingredients in a bowl.
- Form relatively thick patties of the desired size.
- Fry them in plenty of butter.
- Make a sauce with the pan drippings.
- Pour a cup of water into the skillet.
- Crumble a beef bouillon cube over it.
- Add the liquid from the pickled beets and a few drops of liquid from the capers and let it come to a boil. Pour the sauce over the beef patties.

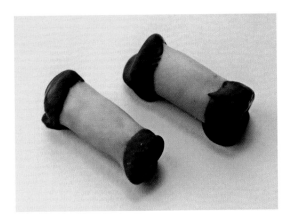

"Vacuum Cleaners"

In all Swedish cafes and bakeries you can find "vacuum cleaners," or punsch rolls, which is their true name. It is said that they are jokingly called vacuum cleaners because they look like old-fashioned vacuum cleaners, and, not only that – the filling is actually made out of old cookies.

Makes 15-20

1 1/2 cups crumbled cookies
4 oz butter or margarine
1/2 cup powdered sugar
1/2 tsp. vanilla extract
1-2 tbsp. cocoa. This is not needed if the cookies you use contain cocoa.
rum or punsch, (see recipe, p. 23), according to preference
7 oz marzipan
1 drop green food coloring
4 oz dark chocolate

- Finely crumble the cookies in a food processor or by hand.
- Combine the butter or margarine, powdered sugar, vanilla extract and cocoa (if needed), in a mixing bowl.
- Add the crumbled cookies.
- Flavor the mixture with punsch or rum to taste.
- Color the marzipan with a drop of green food coloring. A tip is to place the marzipan on plastic wrap and then knead the marzipan so it becomes evenly colored green.
- Thinly roll out the marzipan. This is easier if done on plastic wrap.
- Cut out squares of marzipan measuring approximately 2 1/2 inches.
- Place a good-sized mound of the cookie-crumb mixture on each marzipan square and roll them up.
- When the rolls are complete, melt the chocolate in the microwave or a double boiler.
- Dip the ends of each roll in the chocolate.
- Place them on a sheet of wax paper to set.

Chocolate Biscuits and Sarah Bernhardts

Chocolate biscuits were one of my favorite treats growing up. I especially liked the ones that had a little piece of paper with the name "Sarah Bernhardt" written on it and stuck in their chocolate tops. Later, I learned that the difference between Sarah Berhardts and regular chocolate biscuits was on the inside: Sarah

Bernhardts had chocolate truffle filling and regular chocolate biscuits had butter cream.

So how did it happen that the French prima donna, Sarah Bernhardt, became better known in Sweden as a chocolate biscuit than as an actress? Well, in 1911, the French actress made a highly celebrated visit to Copenhagen. Johannes Steen, pastry chef and owner of Steen's Konditori on Amager Torv, was assigned the task of coming up with something special to commemorate her arrival. This lovely almond biscuit with chocolate truffle filling and a chocolate glaze was the delicious result. He couldn't have done better.

Makes 15

Bases

> 2/3 cup almonds
> 2/3 cup sugar
> 2 egg whites
> or
> 6 oz almond paste
> 1 egg white

Oven temperature: 350° F

- Blanche and grind the almonds.
- Combine the almonds and sugar or use ready-made almond paste and add an egg white.
- Lay out 15 small mounds on a baking sheet covered with baking parchment or buttered.
- Bake them on the middle rack of the oven 5-10 minutes.
- Remove the cookies from the baking sheet right away and let cool.

Garnish

8 oz dark chocolate
1 tbsp. cooking oil

Filling

Alternative 1
Butter cream filling

4 oz butter
1/2 cup powdered sugar
1 egg yolk
2 tbsp. cocoa

- Mix the butter and sugar until soft.
- Add the egg yolk and cocoa. Stir.
- Spread the butter cream on the almond bases.
- Place them in the freezer for about 20 minutes to set.
- Melt chocolate, to be used for dipping, in double boiler or microwave and add the cooking oil.
- Dip chilled cookies in melted chocolate.

Alternative 2
Chocolate truffle filling

3 oz dark chocolate
1 tbsp. butter
2 tbsp. heavy cream

- Melt the chocolate in the double boiler.
- Melt the butter in a saucepan. Add the cream.
- Pour the butter-cream mixture into the chocolate while beating hard.
- Let the mixture stand and cool so that it thickens.
- Spread the mixture onto the almond cookies, forming a peak on each.
- Place them in the refrigerator for about an hour.
- Melt chocolate, to be used for dipping, in double boiler or microwave and add the cooking oil.
- Dip the cookies quickly in the chocolate mixture so that the filling is covered.
- Return cookies to fridge and let the chocolate coating harden.
- You can even keep the cookies in the freezer until serving time.

Mazarin Tarts

The mazarin tart has been around for almost 400 years. Its orgin can be traced to France, where there was a cardinal and statesman, Jules Mazarin, who led the government until Louis XVI came of age. This Mr. Mazarin loved sweets, and he was especially fond of a glazed tart made of butter pastry with almond filling. Mazarin tarts made its way to Sweden and the entire Swedish people learned to love this pastry.

18-20 tarts

1 1/4 cups all-purpose flour
3 1/2 tbsp. sugar
1/2 tsp. baking powder
4 oz butter or margarine
1 egg (small)

Filling

1 cup almonds
4 oz butter or margarine
3 eggs
2/3 cup sugar

Garnish

1 cup powdered sugar + a few drops water

Oven temperature: 400° F

- Butter muffin tins (disposable aluminum muffin tins work fine too).
- Combine the flour and baking powder in a mixing bowl.
- Add the sugar, butter and egg.
- Mix until it forms a flaky dough.
- Let dough stand in the refrigerator and rest for a while, approx. 60 minutes.
- Line the muffin tins with the pastry dough.

For the filling:
- Blanche, peel and grind the almonds.
- Melt the butter or margarine.
- Beat the egg and sugar until fluffy. Stir in the melted butter or margarine and the ground almonds.
- Add filling to the pastry.
- Bake on the middle or lower rack of the oven about 15 minutes.
- Let the tarts cool.
- Wet the powdered sugar with a few drops of water to make a glaze and spread over the tarts.

BEEF ROULADES

1 lb boneless beef round steak, sliced thin
1 tsp. salt
10 allspice corns
2 tsp. whole black pepper corns
1 1/2 tbsp. butter or margarine
1 cup water
2 tbsp. all-purpose flour
1/2 cup whole milk or heavy cream

Suggested fillings:
Smoked ham or bacon and mustard
Pickled cucumbers, mustard and finely chopped red onion
Mustard, finely chopped red onion, beets and pickled cucumbers

- Prepare the desired filling.
- Flatten the meat with a mallet. The roulades should measure about 6" x 3".
- Place a little bit of filling on top and roll up the meat.
- Secure the meat with a toothpick or cotton thread.
- Brown the meat on all sides in a frying pan with butter.
- Place the meat in a pot, preferably large enough to lay all the roulades on the bottom.
- Crush the black pepper and allspice with a mortar and pestle and sprinkle over roulades.
- Add salt, then the water.
- Cover with lid and let the roulades braise over low heat for about 30-40 minutes. If necessary add more water.
- Remove roulades from pan and discard the thread or toothpicks.
- Strain the pan juices into a saucepan.
- Combine flour and milk, then whisk into the pan to thicken the juices.
- Let the gravy simmer until it reaches the desired consistency.
- Pour the gravy over the roulades.
- Serve with boiled or riced potatoes.

MASHED TURNIP WITH BOILED PORK

Mashed turnip with boiled pork is a good old-fashioned meal that has remained popular throughout the years. Turnip was one of the most important vegetables people grew, especially before the potato arrived—gardens were jokingly called turnip gardens. Turnip was filling and kept well in the earth cellars during the entire long winter.

Boiled Pork

3 lb fresh pork shoulder
3 quarts water
3 tsp. salt
1/4 tsp. ground white pepper
1 small yellow onion, coarsely chopped
1 bay leaf
4 allspice corns

- Bring water to a boil and add all the ingredients.
- Cover and simmer over low heat about 2 hours, or until the meat is cooked through. Cooking time will vary a bit, depending on the size of the meat.
- Reserve about 1/3-1/2 cup stock.

Mashed Turnip

2 quarts water
turnip, about 2 lb
3 carrots
7 potatoes
1-2 tsp. salt
1/3-1/2 cup pork stock

- Cut the turnip into small pieces.
- Bring water to a boil and add the salt. Add turnip and boil for 30 minutes.
- Cut the carrots and potatoes into small pieces and add them too. Cook until soft.
- Pour off the water. Add 1/3 cup of the stock from the pork shoulder or the stock from cooking the vegetables and mash.
- Serve with the boiled pork, a little stock and mustard.

SWEDISH HASH

Nighttime snack or lunch dish, Swedish hash tastes good anytime of the day or night accompanied by fried eggs and beets. In school we used to jokingly call the dish "the week in review," since people often assemble whatever leftovers are on hand to throw into a pot of Swedish hash.

1 lb boneless beef
2 medium yellow onions
8 medium potatoes
2 tbsp. margarine
1 tsp. salt
a pinch of freshly ground
black pepper

- Cut the beef into small cubes.
- Peel and cut the potatoes into small cubes.
- Peel and finely chop the onion.
- Sauté the potatoes first (in two batches, if necessary) so they are cooked through but still firm. Put sautéed potatoes in a large pan and cover with lid to keep warm.
- Then sauté the onions and add them to the pot.
- Lastly, sauté the meat and add to pot. Reserve pan juices in a cup.
- Add the pan juices to the pot. Season with salt and pepper.
- Serve with fried eggs and pickled beets (see recipe, p. 30)

PAN BEEF WITH ONIONS

Pan beef is akin to large meatballs or a Swedish variation of the hamburger.

1 lb ground beef (or half ground beef, half ground pork)
3-4 medium yellow onions
1 tsp. salt
a pinch of white- or black pepper

butter or margarine for frying

- Peel and slice the onion.
- Brown the onions in the frying pan over low heat until they are soft. If the frying pan is small brown onions in two batches.
- Salt and pepper the ground meat and mix well with your hands.
- Form 4-8 beef patties depending on the size desired.
- Fry the patties in a pan. Cover with a lid so they get cooked through completely.
- After cooking the last patty, add approximately 1/2 cup of water to the pan. Cook to release pan juices.
- Serve the patties with fried onions, boiled potatoes and carrots and a little lingonberry preserves.

KALOPS

The word kalops comes from the British "collops", which means sliced meat. And, as the word indicates, this dish is made up of strips of meat. Kalops has its roots in the southern part of Sweden and is eaten with pickled beets.

1 1/2 lb beef stew meat
2 tbsp. butter
2 yellow onions
2 peeled carrots cut into chunks
1 1/2 tsp. salt
5 allspice corns
a pinch of white pepper
3 bay leaves
2-2 1/2 cups water
2 tbsp. all-purpose flour

- Peel and cut the onions into wedges.
- Cut the beef into slices or chunks.
- Melt the butter in a pan. Add beef and brown on all sides.
- Add the onions and cook for a little while.
- Transfer beef and onions to a stew pot.
- Season with salt, pepper, allspice and bay leaves. Add the water.
- Cover and braise over low heat until meat is tender, about 40-60 minutes.
- Add carrots when the meat has cooked for 30 minutes.
- When the meat is tender, mix the flour with a little water. Pour over the stew and cook for 3-5 minutes while stirring.
- Serve with potatoes and pickled beets (see recipe, p. 30).

OVEN-BAKED
PORK PANCAKE

Ironically, this is equally good with or without the pork. It appeals to younger diners and makes a great dinner for the whole family.

> 3 1/3 cups whole milk
> 1 2/3 cups all-purpose flour
> 2 eggs
> 1/2 tsp. salt
> 1 tbsp. butter
> 8 oz bacon or pork

Oven temperature: 425° F

- Beat together the eggs and half the milk.
- Add the flour and salt. Beat batter until smooth.
- Add in the rest of the milk.
- Chop the bacon or pork into small pieces, then fry in their own fat.
- Butter a roasting pan or two ovenproof dishes.
- Add the meat to the pan. Pour the pancake batter over the meat and mix with fork.
- Bake until the pancake is golden brown, approx 20-30 minutes.
- Serve with lingonberry preserves.

SHOEMAKER'S DISH

This Swedish classic is often served for lunch in restaurants. Actually, it is a rather curious dish, made up of sirloin steak topped with fried bacon and onions, served with mashed potatoes. The sirloin steak looks a great deal like the sole of a shoe, which is probably why the dish is dedicated to shoemakers.

1-1.5 lb thin slices of sirloin steak
6 oz bacon
1 large yellow onion
butter or margarine for sautéing
salt and white pepper
chives

Mashed Potatoes

10-12 potatoes
water and salt
2 tbsp. butter
approx 1 cup whole milk
salt, white pepper and a dash of
freshly ground nutmeg

- Peel and boil the potatoes.
- Finely chop the onion.
- Slice the bacon into thin strips.

- Brown the bacon and onion.
- When the potatoes are cooked, pour off the water. Mash them and add the butter.
- Add milk until the desired consistency is reached.
- Season with salt, white pepper and freshly ground nutmeg.
- Brown the sirloin in butter, 2-3 minutes on each side. It should be a little pink inside.
- Transfer to a plate and cover with browned onions and bacon. Serve with a side of mashed potatoes. Decorate with chives.
- If pan juices are desired, pour a little water into the frying pan and boil quickly to release them.

BAKED MACARONI

This Swedish variation of macaroni and cheese is well loved, especially by children.

1 2/3 cups plain macaroni pasta
6 cups water
1/2 lb. beef frankfurters or ham
1 1/4 cup whole milk
2 eggs
1/4 cup grated cheese
1 tbsp. butter
1 tsp. salt (1/2 tsp. for boiling the macaroni, 1/2 tsp. for the dish)
black pepper

Oven temperature: 425° F

- Cook macaroni according to the package directions; make sure to use 1/2 tsp. salt in the water.
- Chop the frankfurters or cube the ham and brown lightly in the butter.
- Mix together the cooked macaroni with the frankfurters.
- Transfer to buttered oven-proof dish.
- Beat egg and milk and pour over macaroni mixture.
- Add salt and pepper.
- Sprinkle with the grated cheese.
- Bake until the pudding is set and golden brown.

PRUNE-LARDED PORK ROAST

If we didn't eat steak on Sundays, prune-larded pork roast was often on the menu. It makes a festive meal for when the entire family gathers around the dining room table.

2 1/2- 3 lb fresh boneless center cut pork or fresh pork roast
8-10 pitted prunes
salt
black pepper
approximately 1 1/2 cups water to baste the pork with during roasting

For the gravy:
1 tbsp. flour
a little milk

Oven temperature: 350° F

- Butter an ovenproof dish.
- Make small incisions in the pork roast and stuff in the prunes. Place roast in the ovenproof dish.
- Salt and pepper the roast on all sides.
- Insert a meat thermometer.
- Cover entire dish with aluminum foil. Place it in the oven.
- After about 15 minutes, baste the roast with a little water. Repeat regularly so the roast doesn't dry out or burn. Use a little extra water during the last hour as it will act as a base for the gravy.
- When the meat thermometer registers 175° F the roast is done.
- Make gravy out of the pan juices by whisking in approximately 1 tbsp. flour. If desired, add a little milk. Season to taste with salt and pepper.
- Slice the roast and lay the slices on a serving platter. Garnish with the extra prunes.
- The dish tastes best with boiled potatoes and a little applesauce. Serve with some boiled vegetables as well.

All Saints' and Martin Goose Day

▸▸ Similar to the U.S., where we celebrate All Saints' Day with Halloween on October 31st, in Sweden All Saints' Day falls on the first weekend in November. The Swedes, however, don't usually celebrate the holiday with quite as much playfulness. Lately, people have been influenced by the American way, and children dress themselves up as monsters and such. Personally, I remember the holiday as dismal. Everything was black and boring. I'll never forget when we traveled to Norrköping one All Saints' Day to stay in a motel, which was an exciting event for a five-year-old. Disappointment occurred promptly when it became clear to me that everything was closed, including the toy stores. I loved to shop in toy stores, and could spend hours looking at everything that was there. Saturday was most often the day that I could do that so Saturday quickly became my favorite day, in contrast to boring Sunday when everything was closed. My assessment of All Saints' Weekend was that it consisted not of one Sunday but of two. So, All Saints' Day was not my favorite holiday as a child. One thing I did like was the atmosphere created in the churchyard by the candles we'd light for our ancestors. Swedes imported that custom from the continent in the 1920s.

All Saints' Day falls on the first Saturday in November. In the beginning it was celebrated on November 1st. The day was created in the 800s because there were no longer enough calendar days on which to celebrate each individual saint. Therefore, the Pope instituted a day for all saints so that nobody would be forgotten. The day after became the day when people devoted their attention to all the other souls. The living would honor the rest of dead, those who weren't saints or martyrs.

As I said, All Saints' Day was a pretty boring day for a child. It wasn't until I came to New York and celebrated Halloween that I developed a new take on the holiday. I really got a taste of the festive quality after dressing up and walking in the Halloween parade along Sixth Avenue. It was something I'll remember all my life, and I am careful to relive each year with our daughter – she loves Halloween and begins to wonder as soon as the pumpkins show up at the farmer's market in Union Square what costume she'll choose this year.

Thanksgiving, for obvious reasons, is not a holiday that is celebrated in Sweden, even if we've been good at picking up American customs. But November 10th is Martin Goose Day, or St. Martin's Eve, as people in the southern province of Skåne call the day. The Martin they mean to celebrate is Bishop Martin of Tours, who was a heathen soldier in the 300s. St. Martin's Day falls on November 11th, but as is the custom in Sweden, it is the evening before that is important. The reason that Martin of Tours came to be associated with geese is that he tried to avoid becoming Bishop by hiding in a goose pen. The loud honking of the geese gave away his hiding place and because of this he decided to have them all slaughtered. Martin of Tours became Bishop and, eventually, the patron saint of France. The tradition of eating goose on St. Martin's Day is common on the continent and the custom spread all the way up to Sweden. At this time of year the geese are ready for slaughtering, fat enough after having eaten spilled grain in the fields. This has surely helped the people of Skåne, a province of southern Sweden, to celebrate the day.

In our home we would substitute turkey for goose but otherwise we dined in the true style of Skåne. It was a festive meal and the food lasted several days; turkey is known for its leftovers. In older times, goose was eaten in homes all the way up to Norrland, and those homes that couldn't afford goose made a festive meal with duck or chicken instead.

Black soup is part of a true goose dinner. This custom appears to be relatively young, barely two hundred years, and has its origin at a restaurant in Stockholm. Black soup is made from goose blood, bouillon, cooked apples, vinegar, and a large number of spices.

When people say "goose" in Sweden their thoughts are drawn either to Martin Goose Day or to one of the country's most beloved books, the *Marvelous Adventures of Nils Holgersson*. The book is about a little boy, Nils, who went with the goose, Akaa, on a journey around the country. From the back of the goose he could look out over the landscape of Sweden and see everything that our beautiful oblong country has to offer. The author, Selma Lagerlöf, was one of the few women and few Swedes to receive the Nobel Prize for literature. The book was used to teach geography in the schools for many years. Selma Lagerlöf lived in Värmland in a manor called Mårbacka. My husband has roots not very far from there, and it's a place which I have gotten to know very well over the years.

After Martin Goose Day, Father's Day is celebrated on the second Sunday of November, the last holiday before long-awaited Christmas knocks at the door. Christmas is the year's most beloved holiday for Swedes, and is celebrated for several weeks – I devoted an entire previous book to the Swedish Christmas alone! After Christmas, only New Year's remains. This is a day that has become the big day of shellfish, champagne, and fireworks. But it is also a day when the past year will be summed up and new expectations will be created for a wonderful new year with many, many wonderful memories to be added to the long journey of life.

ST. MARTIN'S GOOSE

St. Martin's Goose Day falls in the middle of autumn when darkness has come to stay. It is celebrated especially widely in Skåne, Sweden's southernmost province. They eat a special goose dinner. In my home we had turkey, which, in my opinion, tastes just as good.

1 turkey or goose – choose the size according to the number of guests

Filling:
juice of 1/2 lemon
2-3 tart apples
1 bunch of parsley
8 oz pitted prunes
salt and pepper

Oven temperature: 350° F

For the stuffing:
- Peel and slice apples and mix with the prunes and chopped parsley.

For the fowl:
- Butter a roasting pan or an adequately large disposable foil pan.
- Place the turkey of goose breast side up in the pan. Remove the innards.
- Brush the cavity with lemon juice then add the stuffing.
- Sew together the opening with needle and thread so the stuffing won't fall out.
- Season with desired amount of salt and pepper.
- Loosely cover the bird with aluminum foil.

- Estimate cooking time, 15-20 minutes per pound.
- Pour a little water in the roasting pan after about 10 minutes of cooking. Continue adding water as needed so the bird doesn't dry out.
- Remove the foil after half the roasting time has elapsed and baste regularly with the juices to give the turkey or goose a beautiful golden-brown appearance.
- When the bird is done roasting, take it out of the oven and cover again with the foil to keep it warm.

Gravy:
- Strain the pan juices into a saucepan.
- Bring them to a boil.
- Mix 1-2 tbsp. flour in a little water and whisk into the pan juices.
- Simmer over low heat for 5 minutes, stirring constantly.
- Add either milk or cream, as desired.
- Season to taste with salt, pepper, and, if desired, a little soy sauce.

Red Cabbage

Red cabbage takes a little time to make, so it's best to start while the turkey or goose is cooking.

Serves 6-8 people

3 1/2 lb red cabbage
butter or margarine
1/4-1/2 cup corn syrup
3 apples
3 tbsp. red vinegar
1 tbsp. salt
1/2 -1 tsp. black pepper
1/4 cup red wine

- Slice the cabbage into very fine strips.
- Peel, core and cut the apples.
- Melt the butter.
- Add the cabbage to the pan, alternating with the corn syrup.
- Sauté briefly, stirring constantly.
- Add the apples and vinegar to the pan.
- Cover and simmer for about 40-60 minutes, stirring every now and then to keep the cabbage from sticking.
- Season with the salt, pepper and red wine.

Cooked Apples with Grape Jelly

- Peel, core and halve desired number of apples.
- Boil a few minutes in lightly sugared water until slightly soft.
- Let the apples cool and then fill the halves with grape jelly.

Browned Potato Wedges

- Cut the desired number of potatoes into wedges.
- Boil but remove them from the heat while still a little hard.
- Dredge wedges in dried breadcrumbs.
- Saute in butter until golden brown.

Brussels sprouts and applesauce complete the traditional side dishes for goose dinner.

CANNED PEARS IN GINGER

My grandmother was a master at canning pears in ginger. To my great delight my own canned pears turned out almost as well as hers. That's not so strange, really, considering that I used her recipe.

8 average-sized pears (more if you use small pears)
2 cups water
1 1/2 cups sugar
2-3 pieces of fresh ginger (approx. 1 inch each)

- Peel the pears but do not core.
- Dissolve sugar in boiling water, stirring constantly.
- Turn heat down to low and add pears and ginger. Simmer until very soft.
- Transfer pears and syrup to a glass jar with an airtight lid.
- Store in the fridge or eat them right a way with a dollop of whipped cream.

SHELLFISH

At no other time of year is so much shellfish, especially lobster, eaten as on New Year's Eve. If you visit Gothenburg or the West Coast of Sweden, however, you should certainly indulge in the shellfish any time of year, for that is where they really understand the art of preparing fish.

Lobster

For three lobsters

4 quarts water
1/2 cup salt
3 tsp. sugar
1 tsp. caraway seeds
Optional: 1/2 -1 cup dill

- Combine all ingredients and bring to a boil. Add the lobsters and cook for 15-20 minutes, depending on size.

Stone Crab

Same procedure as for lobster but omit the dill.

Mussels

approximately 40 blue mussels
1/2 cup water

1 cup white wine
1 fish bouillon cube
a pinch of white pepper
1 yellow onion
heavy cream (optional)

- Scrape, brush and rinse the mussels thoroughly.
Finely chop the onion.
Bring water to a boil in a stock pot and add onion and fish bouillon cube.
- Add mussels to the boiling water and boil, covered, 4-6 minutes until mussels have opened.
- Add wine and season with white pepper. Add cream, if desired. This creates a tasty sauce, perfect for dipping bread.
- Mussels that haven't opened should be removed before serving.

MEASUREMENTS AND CONVERSIONS

Conversions of US Liquid measures to nearest metric:

1/2 tsp	= 2.5 ml
1 tsp	= 5 ml
1/2 tbsp	= 7.5 ml
1 tbsp	= 15 ml
1/4 cup	= 2 fluid oz
	= 60 ml
1/3 cup	= 2/6 fluid oz
	= 80 ml
1/2 cup	= 4 fluid oz
	= 120 ml
2/3 cup	= 5/3 fluid oz
	= 160 ml
3/4 cup	= 6 fluid oz
	= 180 ml
1 cup	= 8 fluid oz
	= 16 tbsp
	= 240 ml
1 pint	= 20 fluid oz
	= 600 ml
1 quart	= 33/8 fluid oz
	= 1000 ml
1 cup UK	= 10 fluid oz
	= 295 ml

Conversions of US Weight measure to nearest gram:

4 oz	= 1/4 lb
	= 112 g
8 oz	= 1/2 lb
	= 224 g
12 oz	= 3/4 lb
	= 336 g
16 oz	= 1 lb
	= 448 g
32 oz	= 2 lb
	= 896 g

Conversions of US length measure to nearest centimeter:

1/4 inch	= 0.6 cm
1/2 inch	= 1.2 cm
1 inch	= 2.5 cm
12 inch	= 1 foot
	= 30 cm

Approx. Oven Temperatures:

275°F	= 135°C
300°F	= 150°C
325°F	= 165°C
350°F	= 175°C
375°F	= 190°C
400°F	= 200°C
425°F	= 220°C
450°F	= 230°C
475°F	= 245°C
500°F	= 260°C

INDEX OF RECIPES

Agneta's U.S.A. Cake 144
Almond Cake 140
Aniseed, Fennel and Caraway Schnapps 121
Apple Pie 173

Baked Macaroni 209
Baked Potatoes with Shrimp Skagen 36
Baltic Herring with Mashed Potatoes 131
Beef à la Lindström 190
Beef Roulades 197
Beef Rydberg 88
Beefsteak with Onions 67
Berry Schnapps 121
Brown Beans with Salt Pork 183

Cabbage Soup with Quenelles 185
Canned Pears in Ginger 219
Chocolate Biscuits and Sarah Bernhardts 192
Cinnamon Buns 174
Cod with Egg Sauce 86
Cod with Horseradish 127
Crayfish 162

Dill and Coriander Schnapps 121

Egg Sandwich with Matjes Herring 32
Egg Toddy 59

Fish Roe Herring 116

Gentlemen's Delight 41
Gotland Saffron Pancake 128
Grandmother's Pickled Pressed Cucumbers 72
Hasselback Potatoes 72
Herring à la Russe 116

Hollandaise Sauce 122
Horseradish Herring 116

Kalops 203
King's Meringues 75

Leg of Lamb with Potatoes au Gratin 56
Lemon Balm Schnapps 121
Lenten Buns 12
Lobster 220

Mashed Potatoes 35, 206
Mashed Turnip with Boiled Pork 198
Matjes Herring Torte 119
Mazarin Tarts 195
Meat with Dill Sauce 26
Meatball Sandwich with Reed Beet Salad 31
Meatballs with Cream Gravy 34
Mildly Cured Lax with Potatoes and
    Dill Sauce 94
Mussels 220

Oven-Baked Pork Pancake 205

Pan Beef with Onions 201
Pea Soup 22
Pickled Baltic Herring 131
Pickled Beets 30
Pickled Herring 114
Pinocchio Cake 136
Poached Salmon 122
Potato Dumplings 177
Potato Cakes 90
Potato Leek Soup 151
Potato Pancakes 124
Potatoes au Gratin 56
Princess Torte 134
Prune-Larded Pork Roast 210
Punsch 23

Red Beet Salad 31
Red Cabbage 217
Rhubarb Cream 40
Rhubarb Pie 38
Royal Pot Roast 71

Saft – Fruit Syrup Drink 147
Sailor's Beef 181
Salmon Pudding 153
Salmon Trout with Fish Roe Sauce 189
Salt Pork with Onion Sauce 182
Sautéed Salmon with Spinach 93
Schnapps 120
Sharp Sauce 122
Shellfish 220
Shoemaker's Dish 206
Shrimp Sandwich 28
Småland Cheesecake 178
St. Martin's Goose 216
Stone Crab 220
Strawberry Cake 143
Stuffed Cabbage Rolls 186
Swedish Hash 200
Swedish Pancakes 25
Swedish Sandwiches 28

Sweet Limpa Bread 32

Tomato Herring 116
Tosca Cake 139

Vacuum Cleaners 192
Waffles 46
Wallenbergers 64
Vanilla Sauce 173
Vanilla Schnapps 121
Vegetable Soup 148
West Coast Salad 97
White Wine Sauce 123